Chartered Institute for Securities & Investment

Level 3

Certificate in Corporate Finance

Unit 1 – Regulation

Practice & Revision Kit

Syllabus version 13

Published March 2018

ISBN 9781 5097 1603 6

British Library Cataloguing-in-Publication Data
A catalogue record for this book
is available from the British Library

Published by

BPP Learning Media Ltd
BPP House, Aldine Place
London W12 8AA

www.bpp.com/learningmedia

Printed in the United Kingdom

Your learning materials, published by BPP Learning Media Ltd, are
printed on paper obtained from traceable sustainable sources.

BPP
LEARNING MEDIA

Question Bank

Contents

Unit 1 – Regulation

The Regulatory Environment in the UK

Questions

1. **The following are all classified as specified investments within the Regulated Activities Order, except:**

    A ADRs

    B Life assurance policies

    C Electronic money

    D Currencies

2. **Which of the following is the strategic objective of the Financial Conduct Authority?**

    A To protect and enhance the integrity of the UK financial system

    B To promote effective competition in the interests of consumers

    C To ensure that the relevant markets function well

    D To secure an appropriate degree of protection for consumers

3. **Which of the following is a means of obtaining authorisation to carry out a regulated activity in the UK?**

    A Application to the Financial Conduct Authority

    B Direct application to Securities and Exchange Commission

    C Application to a designated professional body

    D Membership of a Recognised Investment Exchange

4. **Which of the following are specified investments covered by the Regulated Activities Order?**

    I ADRs

    II CDs

    III Premium bonds

    IV Bank loans

    A I, II, III and IV

    B I, II and IV

    C I and II

    D II and III

5. **Which one of the following would not be regarded as carrying out an investment business under FSMA?**

    A Arranging deals in investments

    B Advising on investments in a *Financial Times* column

    C Publishing a Tip Sheet

    D Giving advice on investments as a trustee

6. All of the following are RIEs, except:

A London Stock Exchange

B Euronext London

C New York Stock Exchange

D London Metal Exchange

7. All of the following are specified investments, except:

A Bulldog bonds

B Certificates of Deposit

C Units of a unit trust which invests in tangible property

D Futures contracts entered into for commercial purposes

8. What is the maximum penalty for conducting unauthorised investment business?

A Six months' imprisonment and/or a fine of £5,000

B Two years' imprisonment and/or a fine of £5,000

C Six months' imprisonment and/or an unlimited fine

D Two years' imprisonment and/or an unlimited fine

9. Which Principle for Businesses compels firms to have risk management systems in place?

A Management and Control

B Conflicts of Interest

C Market Conduct

D Maintaining Controls

10. Which of the following is not correct regarding the nature of the Regulatory Decisions Committee?

A All RDC members are FCA employees

B The RDC can decide to refuse an application for Part 4A permission

C The RDC committee is part of the FCA

D The RDC is not a part of the FCA's executive management

11. Under MiFID which of the following is correct?

A Where a passported MiFID branch conduct of business takes place with host state residents, then home state rules apply

B Authorisation is granted by the host state in each case

C MiFID applies to activities related to all possible investments

D Home state conduct of business rules apply for services given to residents in another EEA member state

12. **An inspector to investigate companies' affairs may be appointed under which of the following circumstances?**

    I   By appointment of the Chancellor of the Exchequer

    II   By holders of at least 5% of issued shares

    III By the company itself after passing an ordinary resolution

    IV By at least 20 members

A I only

B III only

C II and IV only

D I, II, III and IV

13. **All of the following would be covered under the 'governing function' category of controlled functions, except:**

A Chief executive

B Director

C Managing a specific product

D Non-executive director

14. **Which are the two statutory objectives of the Prudential Regulation Authority?**

    I   (Specifically for insurers) to contribute to the securing of an appropriate degree of protection for policy holders

    II   Protect and enhance the integrity of the UK financial system

    III To promote the safety and soundness of the firms it regulates

    IV Secure an appropriate degree of protection for consumers

A I and IV

B II and III

C I and III

D II and IV

15. **Which of the following would not be exempt from authorisation?**

A The London Metal Exchange

B An issuer of e-money

C The International Monetary Fund

D Bank of England

16. **Which of the following is not classed as a MiFID core activity?**

A Portfolio management

B Safekeeping and administration of financial instruments for client accounts

C Investment advice

D Operating a multilateral trading facility

17. **MiFID does not cover which of the following instruments?**

A   Forex swaps

B   Equities

C   ADRs

D   Property

18. **The body which could be best described as focusing on the stability of the whole financial system, focusing on large international banks is the:**

A   Financial Conduct Authority

B   London Stock Exchange

C   HM Treasury

D   Prudential Regulation Authority

19. **Allowing a firm to undertake specific business activities is most accurately described as the granting of:**

A   Authorisation

B   FSMA 2000 consent

C   Exemption

D   Part 4A permission

20. **Section 165 of the FSMA 200 gives the Financial Conduct Authority statutory powers to require that a firm provide it with specified information or documents within what time period?**

A   Immediately

B   A reasonable timescale as prescribed by the FCA

C   Within two business days

D   At the convenience of the firm

21. **All of the following are controlled functions under SUP 10, except:**

A   Compliance function

B   Chief executive

C   Company secretary

D   Customer function

22. **When assessing an individual's fitness and propriety for the Financial Conduct Authority approved person regime, the FCA is least likely to take account of which factor?**

A   A person's financial soundness

B   A person's personal wealth

C   A person's competence and capability

D   A person's honesty, integrity and reputation

23. **Individuals undertaking a controlled function are known as:**

   A   Appointed representatives

   B   Independent Financial Advisers

   C   Approved persons

   D   Authorised persons

24. **All of the following are criteria when assessing an individual's fitness and propriety, except:**

   A   Age

   B   Competence and capability

   C   Integrity

   D   Financial soundness

25. **Which two of the following best describes the Regulatory Decisions Committee?**

   I   A committee of the Financial Ombudsman Service

   II   A body appointed by Financial Conduct Authority comprising practitioners and individuals

   III   Responsible for assessing appeals against the Tax and Chancery Chamber of the Upper Tribunal

   IV   Responsible for taking disciplinary action against authorised/approved persons

   A   I and IV

   B   II and IV

   C   I and III

   D   II and III

26. **What is the maximum number of employees permitted to work in an authorised firm's compliance department?**

   A   10

   B   20

   C   50

   D   No maximum

27. **Which two of the following approved persons are allowed to deal for their firms?**

   I   Directors

   II   Managers

   III   Representatives

   IV   Traders

   A   I and II

   B   II and III

   C   I and IV

   D   III and IV

28. **Which of the following is not a Financial Conduct Authority Statutory Notice?**

A   Warning Notice

B   Decision Notice

C   Supervisory Notice

D   Determination Notice

29. **Which of the following is a specified investment?**

A   Premium bonds

B   Trade bills

C   Real estate

D   T-bonds

30. **In order for a person to prove fitness and propriety to get Financial Conduct Authority approval, they must show all of the following, except:**

A   A minimum of two years relevant experience

B   An absence of civil convictions

C   A good reputation

D   Honesty and integrity

31. **Who is responsible for prudential regulation of insurance companies in the UK?**

A   The Prudential Regulation Authority

B   HM Treasury

C   The Financial Conduct Authority

D   The Department for Business, Innovation and Skills

32. **The Financial Conduct Authority is funded by which of the following methods?**

A   Contributions from Treasury

B   Contributions from the Bank of England

C   Contributions from the London Stock Exchange

D   Contributions from authorised firms

33. **The regulated activities of dealing and managing relate to all of the following investments, except:**

A   Shares

B   Bonds

C   Warrants

D   Car insurance

34. Who would normally prosecute a firm for conducting unauthorised regulated activities?

   A Department for Business Innovation and Skills

   B London Stock Exchange

   C Financial Conduct Authority

   D HM Treasury

35. Which of the following is not a specified investment?

   A Rights under an endowment policy

   B A bank deposit with one month's notice

   C An option on Brent Crude oil

   D A sale and repurchase agreement

36. Which of the following is false regarding a Recognised Investment Exchange?

   A Membership confers authorisation to do regulated activities

   B Membership provides access to a marketplace in which buyers and sellers may trade

   C They are recognised by the Financial Conduct Authority

   D They regulate the conduct of participants towards each other via their own exchange rules

37. Which of the following bodies is a part of the Financial Conduct Authority?

   A Tax and Chancery Chamber of the Upper Tribunal

   B Takeover Panel

   C Regulatory Decisions Committee

   D International Capital Markets Association

38. If an adviser carries out unauthorised regulated activities, what are the civil consequences?

   A The contract is void

   B The contract is void from the date of prosecution of the adviser

   C The contract is voidable at the discretion of a court

   D The contract is unenforceable by the party carrying out the unauthorised activity

39. Which controlled function covers the activity of the Money Laundering Reporting Officer?

   A Customer function

   B Required function

   C Systems and controls function

   D Governing function

40. **Which two of the following are Recognised Investment Exchanges?**

    I   Tokyo Stock Exchange

    II   NASDAQ

    III ICE Futures Europe

    IV Euronext

A II and IV

B I and III

C I and IV

D III and IV

41. **Which two of the following are not investments under the Regulated Activities Order?**

    I   Shares

    II   Trade bills

    III Corporate bonds

    IV Premium bonds

A II and IV

B III and IV

C I and II

D I and IV

42. **Which of the following statements concerning the Regulatory Decisions Committee is true?**

A All members of the committee are FCA employees

B It is separate from the management of the FCA

C It is funded by the government

D It is not a part of the FCA

43. **Which one of the following is an RIE?**

A ICE Futures Europe

B New York Stock Exchange

C CME Europe

D Financial Conduct Authority

44. **The following statements are all true of the FCA, except:**

A It must have a system to ensure persons are complying with their obligations when conducting investment business

B Its rules are enforceable by law

C It authorises persons to conduct investment business via the SROs and DPBs

D It has three operational objectives

45. **All of the following are investments under the FSMA 2000, except:**

A American Depositary Receipts

B National Savings Certificates

C Contracts for Difference

D FTSE 100 future

46. **Which of the following is responsible for appointing the head of the Financial Conduct Authority?**

A Prudential Regulation Authority

B Department for Business Innovation and Skills

C HM Treasury

D Bank of England

47. **All of the following are classified as investments under the Financial Services and Markets Act 2000, except:**

A Swaps

B FRAs

C FRNs

D Commercial futures

48. **Which of the following is false in relation to establishing fitness and propriety for an individual applying to FCA for approval?**

A The applicant must satisfy the FCA of fitness and properness

B The FCA decision is based on the contents of the application form only

C The applicant must undertake to follow FCA rules

D The FCA may require the applicant to furnish additional information

49. **All of the following beliefs are grounds for the FCA to take enforcement action, except:**

A A firm may not be fit and proper to carry out investment business

B A firm may commit an act of misconduct in the future

C The exercise of enforcement powers is desirable for the protection of investors

D A firm is intending to expand its operations significantly without consulting the FCA

50. **Which of the following FCA notices would not be described as being statutory?**

A Further Decision Notice

B Final Notice

C Warning Notice

D Decision Notice

51.   Which statement is most correct?

A   The FCA may publicly announce any suggested behaviour about a firm or individual as soon as it receives such information

B   The FCA may publicly announce that it has begun disciplinary proceedings against an individual or firm

C   The FCA may not publicly announce any details of disciplinary proceedings against an individual or firm until proceedings have been concluded

D   The FCA may not publicly announce any details of disciplinary proceedings against an individual or firm unless the individual or firm are found at fault

52.   Which of the following is not an exempt person under the Regulated Activities Order?

A   London Stock Exchange

B   Lloyd's

C   Appointed Representative

D   Member of a Designated Professional Body

53.   Which of the following has ultimate power to grant an employee of an authorised firm permission to undertake a controlled function?

A   A compliance officer

B   A board of directors

C   The Financial Conduct Authority

D   A head of department

54.   Once the FCA has issued a Warning Notice under s 387 of FSMA 2000, under what circumstances can they decide to cease the investigation?

A   Once a Warning Notice has been issued, the investigation must be completed

B   The FCA can cease the investigation at any time with either oral or written notice

C   Proceedings set out in the Warning Notice can be discontinued at any time with written notice

D   Proceedings can only be ceased through the intervention of the Department of Business Enterprise and Regulatory Reform

55.   Which of the following is not a specified investment?

A   Shares in an overseas company

B   Sterling-denominated corporate debt

C   National Savings Certificates

D   Tax-exempt deposit accounts

56. **Which of the following is not a regulated activity?**

A Arranging currency transactions in Indian rupees

B Managing a series of collective investment schemes

C Advising on UK share investments

D Dealing in overseas government debt

57. **Where the FCA undertakes an 'investigation', which of the following is not a punishable offence?**

A Falsifying internal documents relevant to the investigation

B Knowingly providing misleading information

C Failing to attend a prearranged meeting

D Concealing documents relevant to the investigation

58. **Within what timescale do regulated firms have to produce documents required in an investigation?**

A 24 hours

B As soon as is reasonably practicable

C 48 hours

D Five business days

59. **A person who is granted permission under Part 4A of FSMA is permitted to conduct all investment business in which of the following jurisdictions?**

A EEA

B EU

C UK

D Jersey

60. **Which of the following is not exempt from authorisation under FSMA 2000?**

A International Monetary Fund

B London Stock Exchange

C Employee Share Scheme

D Publisher's Tip Sheet

61. **Which of the following statements is true of PRIN 7?**

A Communications to private customers must be clear and fair

B Communications to clients must be clear, fair and not misleading

C Communications to customers must be clear, fair and not misleading

D Communications to customers must be clear and fair

62. **Which of the following statements regarding the FCA is false?**

A   It must have a system to ensure persons are complying with their obligations when conducting investment business

B   Its rules are enforceable at law

C   It authorises persons to conduct regulated activities

D   All its Statements of Principle apply to all approved persons

63. **Which of the following is not one of the Principles for Businesses of the FCA?**

A   Information for clients

B   Clients' assets

C   Financial prudence

D   Conflicts of interest

64. **Which of the following is not a Principle for Businesses?**

A   Integrity

B   Customers: relationships of trust

C   Relations with regulators

D   Customer assets

65. **Responsibility for individuals has been defined by the FCA using:**

A   7 principles backed by a code of practice

B   11 general principles supplemented by a code of practice

C   A code of practice only

D   16 rules and a code of conduct

66. **Under the Senior Management Arrangements, Systems and Controls section of the FCA Handbook, for how long must a firm retain records of the apportionment of management?**

A   Three years from the date of appointment of a member of senior management

B   Five years from the date of resignation of a member of senior management

C   Six years from the date of any change in senior management responsibilities

D   Three years from the date of any reassignment of senior management responsibilities

67. **Which of the following is not one of the Principles for Businesses?**

A   Management and control

B   Customers: relationships of trust

C   Market prudence

D   Relations with regulators

68.   What is general Principle 6 of the Principles for Business?

A   Information on customers

B   Clients' assets

C   Financial prudence

D   Customers' interests

69.   All of the following are Statements of Principle, except:

A   Integrity

B   Independence

C   Skill, care and diligence in management

D   Comply with regulatory requirements

70.   What is the maximum penalty for a breach of s 19 in the Crown Court?

A   Six months and/or £5,000 fine

B   Six months and level 5 fine

C   Two years and/or unlimited fine

D   Two years and a statutory fine

71.   The following are all specified investments under the Financial Services and Markets Act 2000, except:

A   Loan stock

B   Futures for commercial purposes

C   Money market instruments

D   Unit trusts

72.   Passporting of investment business authorisation applies to which firms?

A   Authorised firms

B   MiFID firms

C   Investment firms

D   All firms

73.   Which of the following is not a Recognised Investment Exchange?

A   Euronext

B   London Metal Exchange

C   NEX Exchange

D   Euroclear (UK and Ireland)

74. Conducting unauthorised investment business in the UK is a breach of which of the following statutes?

A Criminal Justice Act 1993

B Investment Business Act 1987

C Financial Services and Markets Act 2000

D Companies Act 2006

75. Which of the following is an excluded activity?

A Managing a hedge fund

B Giving advice in a Tip Sheet

C Dealing in futures

D Acting as an unremunerated trustee

76. Which of the following is not an exempt person?

A Tokyo Stock Exchange

B Lloyd's members

C ICE Futures Europe

D NASDAQ

77. Which of the following are exempt from the requirement to seek authorisation?

    I   LSE

    II   NASDAQ

    III   LCH.Clearnet

    IV   NYSE

A I, II, III and IV

B I, II and III

C IV only

D II and IV

78. Which of the following is not a disciplinary matter for the FCA?

A Breach of Conduct of Business Rule

B Breach of a Prohibition Order

C Failure to observe a Warning Notice

D Failure to observe a Decision Notice

79. **Which of the following are exempt from the requirement to seek authorisation under s 19 FSMA?**

    I   Newspapers giving investment advice

    II   Cable TV programmes giving investment advice

    III   Trustees if they are not separately remunerated

    IV   Members of professional bodies where their main activity is not giving investment advice

    A   I and II

    B   I, II and IV

    C   IV only

    D   I, II, III and IV

80. **Which of the following are sanctions available to the FCA?**

    I   To prevent a person performing a controlled function

    II   To prevent a person working in any area of the financial services industry

    III   Public censures

    IV   Suspension of approval

    A   I, II and IV

    B   I, II, III and IV

    C   II and IV

    D   III and IV

81. **Which of the following statements about insider dealing is false?**

    A   It only relates to unpublished, price sensitive information

    B   Legislation covers unit trusts

    C   It is prosecuted by the FCA

    D   It cannot be prosecuted if information is passed on in the proper course of duties

82. **All of the following are true when contrasting market abuse with insider dealing, except:**

    A   Guilt is based on the balance of probabilities for market abuse rather than beyond reasonable doubt for insider dealing

    B   It should be less difficult for the FCA to prove guilt for market abuse

    C   It should be less difficult to impose a fine for market abuse

    D   Neither market abuse or insider dealing cover commodity derivatives

83. **Where is the legislation on market abuse contained?**

    A   Criminal Justice Act

    B   Proceeds of Crime Act

    C   Companies Act

    D   European Union Market Abuse Regulations

84. Which of the following would not constitute the proceeds of criminal activity for money laundering purposes?

A Efficient tax planning

B Tax evasion

C Forgery

D Drug trafficking

85. To verify that client investment funds are legitimate, a firm should do all of the following, except:

A Check the client's identity

B Check the client's background

C Check police records

D Check with the MLRO

86. Which of the following statements about the Joint Money Laundering Steering Group is true?

A It explains, via guidance notes, how to apply the statutory regulations relating to money laundering

B It is a division of the FCA

C It only applies to non-UK firms passporting into the UK

D They relate to market abuse

87. Which instruments are covered by the Insider Dealing legislation?

I Shares

II Bonds

III Options on shares

IV Depository receipts

A I and II

B I, II, III and IV

C I, II and III

D I, II and IV

88. Inside information is least likely to be supplied by which of the following?

A A director

B An office cleaner

C A customer

D A manager

89. **The Accountability Regime includes all of the following elements except which of the following?**

A   Certification regime

B   Senior managers regime

C   Conduct rules

D   Controlled functions

90. **All of the following are recognised as stages in the money laundering process, except:**

A   The placement of cash into the financial system by opening a bank account

B   Conducting a complex series of financial transactions to separate legitimate from illegitimate funds

C   Undertaking illegal activities to generate funds to be laundered

D   Purchasing income generating financial assets with previously invested illegal funds

91. **Which of the following statements regarding insider dealing is false?**

A   Inside information from a primary source is covered

B   Inside information from a secondary source is covered

C   Trading must occur for an offence to be committed

D   Trading need not occur for an offence to be committed

92. **Which of the following is the maximum penalty for an institution which fails to implement internal reporting procedures in respect of money laundering?**

A   Two years' imprisonment or an unlimited fine

B   Five years' imprisonment and an unlimited fine

C   Two years' imprisonment and an unlimited fine

D   Six months' imprisonment and the statutory fine

93. **Which two of the following penalties may the FCA impose for breaching the market abuse offence?**

   I   Maximum fine of £5,000

   II   Seven years' imprisonment

   III   Public censure

   IV   Discipline of approved persons

A   I and II

B   II and III

C   II and IV

D   III and IV

94.   Insider dealing legislation covers all of the following instruments, except:

A   ADRs

B   FTSE Index futures

C   Warrants

D   A unit in an equity fund

95.   The maximum penalty for insider dealing when convicted in a Magistrates' Court is:

A   Seven years' imprisonment or an unlimited statutory fine

B   Seven years' imprisonment and an unlimited statutory fine

C   Six months' imprisonment and a £5,000 statutory fine

D   Two years' imprisonment and an unlimited statutory fine

96.   All of the following would be an offence under market abuse, except:

A   Making a hostile takeover

B   Dealing in UK shares with inside information

C   Making a misleading statement to distort a market in UK shares

D   Misleading practices in securities trading in the UK

97.   You are an employee of a FCA firm and you suspect that a customer may be involved in money laundering. Which of the following is true?

A   The Chief Executive has responsibility for reporting suspicions to the NCA

B   Money Laundering Reporting Officer must report all suspicions to NCA

C   You must report suspicions to Money Laundering Reporting Officer

D   Your supervisor is responsible for reporting suspicions

98.   All of the following are powers available to the FCA if it has found that a person has engaged in market abuse, except:

A   The FCA may make a public statement that a person has engaged in market abuse

B   The FCA may ask the court to impose a restitution order

C   The FCA may impose a maximum fine of £100,000

D   The FCA may ask the court to impose an injunction

99. **Which of the following is NOT a form of market abuse?**

    A   Insider dealing

    B   Manipulating transactions

    C   Processing proceeds of crime

    D   Disseminating false or misleading information

100. **All of the following are true of insider dealing legislation contained in the Criminal Justice Act 1993, except:**

    A   It is punishable by imprisonment

    B   An insider who discloses inside information (other than in the normal course of business) is committing an offence

    C   UK equities, gilts and related derivatives are all covered by the legislation

    D   The conduct must fall short of the standard expected by a regular market user

101. **All of the following are true in relation to the provisions contained within the FCA's Handbook on Money Laundering, FSMA and the Proceeds of Crime Act, except:**

    A   It is a requirement of firms to properly train their staff in recognising and reporting suspicions of money laundering at least once in every two years

    B   The FCA has a statutory objective to reduce the incidence of financial crime, such as money laundering

    C   A firm has to verify both an individual's identity and their address

    D   A firm is required to retain its records of financial transactions for anti-money laundering purposes for a period of three years

102. **Which one of the following financial instruments would not be covered by insider dealing legislation?**

    A   Debentures

    B   Foreign exchange transactions

    C   Shares

    D   Bonds

103. **Which of the following is false with respect to money laundering?**

    A   Failure to report where an individual knows or suspects money laundering is taking place is a civil offence

    B   Assisting someone in the process of money laundering is an offence with a possible penalty of 14 years' imprisonment and/or an unlimited fine

    C   It relates to various types of activity such as counterfeiting, as well as to drug-related offences

    D   It is a criminal offence not to have procedures in place to identify possible money laundering

104. Under the Criminal Justice Act 1993, insider dealing is:

A Against market practice

B A breach of Stock Exchange rules

C A civil offence

D A criminal offence

105. What is the maximum penalty for an individual under the money laundering legislation?

A 14 years' imprisonment and an unlimited fine

B 5 years' imprisonment and an unlimited fine

C 2 years' imprisonment and an unlimited fine

D 7 years' imprisonment and an unlimited fine

106. All of the following are powers of the FCA when investigating insider dealing, except:

A To take evidence from any person under oath

B The sequestration of funds gained through insider dealing

C To demand the production of documents

D To enter premises in the search for evidence

107. Insider dealing is:

A A criminal offence under FSMA 2000

B A civil offence under MiFID

C A civil offence under the Proceeds of Crime Act 2002

D A criminal offence under the CJA 1993

108. What is the order under which money is laundered into the financial system?

A Placement, Integration, Layering

B Positioning, Layering, Integration

C Positioning, Integration, Layering

D Placement, Layering, Integration

109. To whom should a Money Laundering Reporting Officer normally report a money laundering suspicion?

A Bank of England

B Fraud Squad

C Financial Conduct Authority

D National Crime Agency

110. Which of the following is least likely to be used for insider dealing?

A Shares

B Bonds

C Depository receipts

D Futures over a share index

111. Which of the following statements is true in respect of the Code of Market Conduct?

A It contains guidance on the interpretation of market abuse

B It contains law on market abuse

C It is found in the UK Takeover Code

D It is written by HM Treasury

112. What is the maximum penalty for insider dealing?

A 5 years' imprisonment and an unlimited fine

B 14 years' imprisonment

C An unlimited fine

D 7 years' imprisonment and the statutory fine

113. What is the maximum penalty for a breach of the Misleading Statements and Impressions?

A Unlimited fine

B Five years imprisonment

C Seven years imprisonment and an unlimited fine

D Five years imprisonment and an unlimited fine

114. What is NOT true of the offence of money laundering?

A Maximum penalty for assistance is seven years imprisonment and an unlimited fine

B It relates to the proceeds of any criminal activity

C Legislation covers institutional liability

D It is an offence to tip-off a money launderer

115. What is the correct order of the three stages of money laundering?

A Positioning, Layering, Integration

B Placement, Layering, Integration

C Layering, Integration, Positioning

D Layering, Placement, Integration

116. **What is the maximum penalty in the Crown Court for a breach of the Bribery Act for an individual?**

A   Six months' imprisonment and a £5,000 statutory fine

B   Two years' imprisonment and an unlimited statutory fine

C   Seven years' imprisonment and an unlimited statutory fine

D   Ten years' imprisonment and an unlimited statutory fine

117. **Which of the following is NOT true regarding the Bribery Act?**

A   Offering a financial reward for underperformance constitutes bribery

B   A defence for a commercial organisation would be to show that it has adequate procedures to prevent bribery

C   Requesting a financial reward in return for underperformance constitutes bribery

D   Offences occurring outside the UK by UK citizens are not covered by the Act

118. **How many days' notice are usually required for a private company to call a general meeting?**

A   7 calendar days

B   14 calendar days

C   21 calendar days

D   28 calendar days

119. **How many days' notice are required for an AGM for a public company?**

A   7

B   14

C   21

D   28

120. **The percentage of shareholders of a public company needed to require directors to convene a GM is:**

A   5%

B   10%

C   15%

D   25%

121. **How many persons must be present at an AGM to pass a valid resolution?**

A   2 persons personally present or their proxies

B   5 persons personally present or their proxies

C   10 persons personally present or their proxies

D   100 persons personally present or their proxies

122. **How many days' notice are required for a general meeting to pass a special resolution for a listed company?**

    A 21 business days

    B 14 calendar days

    C 21 calendar days

    D 14 business days

123. **Under which section of the Companies Act 2006 can an Investigation Notice be issued?**

    A Section 793

    B Section 112

    C Section 62

    D Section 47

124. **What percentage of shareholders is required to agree to waive the notice period usually required for general meetings for a public company?**

    A 10%

    B 50%

    C 95%

    D 100%

125. **What is not normal business of an AGM?**

    A Approve dividends

    B Approve significant capital expenditures

    C Appoint directors

    D Appoint auditors

126. **What is the maximum penalty if a private company issues shares to the public in breach of s 755 of Companies Act 2006?**

    A Unlimited fines

    B Six months' imprisonment and/or unlimited fines

    C Two years' imprisonment and/or unlimited fines

    D Five years' imprisonment and/or unlimited fines

127. **All of the following would be found in the Articles of a company, except:**

    A Issued share capital

    B Rules on appointing directors

    C Rights of members

    D Powers, responsibilities and liabilities of directors

128. **Financial assistance is permitted in all of the following circumstances, except:**

    A   A distribution of a dividend

    B   The assistance is incidental to a larger purpose

    C   An indemnity granted against a share purchase

    D   In good faith where financial assistance is not the principal purpose of the transaction

Answers

1. **D** Currencies themselves are not specified investments, only currency futures and options. Electronic money is a specified investment.

   See Chapter 1 Section 1.3.4 of your CISI Workbook

2. **C** The Financial Conduct Authority's **strategic** objective is 'to ensure that the relevant markets function well'. The other three possible answers describe the three **operational** objectives of the FCA.

   See Chapter 1 Section 1.2.2 of your CISI Workbook

3. **A** The SEC is the regulatory body in the US. An RIE **itself** is exempt from authorisation but membership of an RIE does not confer authorisation nor exemption from authorisation. A designated professional body does not grant authorisation.

   See Chapter 1 Section 1.3 of your CISI Workbook

4. **C** Premium bonds are excluded as they are products of the UK's National Savings Bank. Loans are only regulated as investments when mortgages. CDs are Certificates of Deposit.

   See Chapter 1 Section 1.3.4 of your CISI Workbook

5. **B** The **primary purpose** of the *Financial Times* is not that of giving investment advice. A trustee is only exempt if **not being paid for his services**. Investment advice via media outlets are excluded activities.

   See Chapter 1 Section 1.4.2 of your CISI Workbook

6. **C** The New York Stock Exchange is a **DIE**.

   See Chapter 1 Section 1.5.2 of your CISI Workbook

7. **D** Only futures for **investment purposes** and exchange-traded futures are investments.

   See Chapter 1 Section 1.3.4 of your CISI Workbook

8. **D** The offence is referred to as the general prohibition.

   See Chapter 1 Section 1.3.2 of your CISI Workbook

9. **A** Principle 3 (management and control) requires a firm to take reasonable care to organise its affairs effectively with adequate risk management systems.

   See Chapter 1 Section 2.2 of your CISI Workbook

10. **A** The only RDC member who is an FCA employee is the chairman.

    See Chapter 1 Section 2.10.2 of your CISI Workbook

11. **D** While home state rules apply under MiFID where services are provided to members of another EEA member state, host state rules apply for conduct of business offered by a passported MiFID branch.

    See Chapter 1 Section 8.2.4 of your CISI Workbook

12. **B**   Members may apply to the department of Business, Innovation and Skills if there are at least 200 members or holders of at least 10% of issued shares. The company itself may apply as can the secretary of state for BIS.

See Chapter 1 Section 3.4 of your CISI Workbook

13. **C**   Managing a specific product is **not** a governing function.

See Chapter 1 Section 2.6.1 of your CISI Workbook

14. **C**   The Prudential Regulation Authority is part of the Bank of England and has the responsibility for the prudential supervision of banks, building societies, credit unions, insurers and large investment firms. The two incorrect answers apply to the FCA.

See Chapter 1 Section 2.1.2 of your CISI Workbook

15. **B**   The LME is a recognised investment exchange and as such exempt from the need for authorisation. The IMF as a supranational body where the UK is a member is exempt. The BOE is exempt. The issuer of electronic money would not be exempt.

See Chapter 1 Section 1.7 of your CISI Workbook

16. **B**   The safekeeping and administration of financial instruments for client accounts is an ancillary activity under MiFID.

See Chapter 1 Section 8.2.3 of your CISI Workbook

17. **D**   Property bought directly is not regulated under FSMA or MiFID.

See Chapter 1 Section 8.2.5 of your CISI Workbook

18. **D**   The Prudential Regulation Authority focuses on the stability of the system as a whole focusing mainly on large international banks.

See Chapter 1 Section 1.2.3 of your CISI Workbook

19. **D**   Applying to carry out specific activities requires Part 4A permission. As a result of obtaining this, the firm becomes authorised.

See Chapter 1 Section 1.3.1 of your CISI Workbook

20. **B**   The FCA may specify any reasonable format for this material.

See Chapter 1 Section 2.9 of your CISI Workbook

21. **C**   Compliance is a 'required' controlled function. The chief executive is a 'governing' function. The company secretary might also be a director but it is not a controlled function in its own right. SUP 10 is the part of the FCA Handbook that sets out the controlled functions.

See Chapter 1 Section 2.6.1 of your CISI Workbook

22. **B**   A person's personal wealth is unlikely to be considered.

See Chapter 1 Section 2.7 of your CISI Workbook

23. **C**   Authorised persons refer to **firms**, not individuals.

See Chapter 1 Section 1.4 of your CISI Workbook

24. **A**   Age is not considered to be a relevant factor.

See Chapter 1 Section 2.7 of your CISI Workbook

25. **B**   The RDC is not related to the Financial Ombudsman Scheme, which is the FCA's consumer arbitration scheme. The TCCUT hears appeals against RDC decisions, not the other way round.

See Chapter 1 Section 2.10.2 of your CISI Workbook

26. **D**   There is no maximum.

See Chapter 1 Section 4.3.2 of your CISI Workbook

27. **D**   Directors and managers must be **separately approved** for each additional controlled function, eg dealing.

See Chapter 1 Section 2.6 of your CISI Workbook

28. **D**   A Determination Notice is not one of the statutory notices the FCA/RDC can issue.

See Chapter 1 Section 2.10.1 of your CISI Workbook

29. **D**   Premium bonds are National Savings and Investments products and exempt. Trade Bills, such as cheques/bills of exchange, are **excluded** from the definition, as is buying real estate or land. T-bonds (Treasury bonds) are bonds issued by governments that are freely transferable and traded.

See Chapter 1 Section 1.3.4 of your CISI Workbook

30. **A**   Experience is not required in order to be fit and proper.

See Chapter 1 Section 2.7 of your CISI Workbook

31. **A**   The PRA is responsible for the prudential regulation of banks, insurance companies and large investment banks.

See Chapter 1 Section 1.2.3 of your CISI Workbook

32. **D**   Authorised firms pay **levies** and the FCA has a duty to ensure the burdens imposed are proportionate to the benefit. The FCA is not part of the government and, therefore, not funded by them.

See Chapter 1 Section 1.2.2 of your CISI Workbook

33. **D**   Car insurance is not covered by the 'dealing' or 'managing' categories. It is covered by the 'effecting or carrying out contracts for insurance' category which is not part of 'designated investment business'.

See Chapter 1 Section 1.4 of your CISI Workbook

34. **C**   The FCA will prosecute for breaches of s 19 FSMA.

See Chapter 1 Section 1.3 of your CISI Workbook

35. **C**   An option on the Brent Crude future would not have been a specified investment.

See Chapter 1 Section 1.3.4 of your CISI Workbook

36. **A** An RIE is exempt from authorisation. Members of an RIE are not exempt.

See Chapter 1 Section 1.7 of your CISI Workbook

37. **C** The Regulatory Decisions Committee is appointed by the FCA. The TCCUT, the Takeover Panel and the International Capital Market Association, however, are totally independent of the FCA.

See Chapter 1 Section 2.10.2 of your CISI Workbook

38. **D** The investor may enforce or cancel the contract, but the unauthorised party may not enforce the contract.

See Chapter 1 Section 1.3 of your CISI Workbook

39. **B** MLROs are legally required in every financial institution.

See Chapter 1 Section 2.6.1 of your CISI Workbook

40. **D** NASDAQ is classified as an ROIE, and should not be included in the answer, TSE is a DIE.

See Chapter 1 Section 1.2.6 of your CISI Workbook

41. **A** Trade bills will not be considered as tradeable debt (not to be confused with Treasury Bills issued by the Debt Management Office which are tradeable and therefore would be termed an investment). Premium bonds are issued by the UK Government's retail savings bank (National Savings and Investments) and their products are all exempt (this would also include National Savings Certificates).

See Chapter 1 Section 1.3.4 of your CISI Workbook

42. **B** The role of the RDC is separate from that of the FCA surveillance inspectors to provide some level of independence in its decisions. Only the chairman is an FCA employee.

See Chapter 1 Section 2.10.2 of your CISI Workbook

43. **A** ICE Futures Europe is part of the Inter Continental Exchange where energy derivatives trade.

See Chapter 1 Section 1.2.6 of your CISI Workbook

44. **C** With the introduction of FSMA 2000, authorisation is now directly by the FCA (formerly the FSA) and not via the Self Regulatory Organisations or Designated Professional Bodies.

See Chapter 1 Section 1.2.2 of your CISI Workbook

45. **B** National Savings Certificates are part of the government's National Savings and Investments Bank and are therefore exempt.

See Chapter 1 Section 1.3.4 of your CISI Workbook

46. **C** Her Majesty's Treasury is responsible for appointing the FCA's chairman.

See Chapter 1 Section 1.2.4 of your CISI Workbook

47. **D** Forward Rate Agreements (FRAs) are contracts for a difference and Floating Rate Notes (FRNs) are types of bonds. Commercial forwards are excluded from the definition of specified investments as they are not for investment purposes.

See Chapter 1 Section 1.3.4 of your CISI Workbook

48. **B** The FCA has wide powers to assess the fitness and propriety of approved persons, including making its own enquiries beyond the contents of the application form.

See Chapter 1 Section 2.7 of your CISI Workbook

49. **D** The FCA has wide powers to take enforcement action where it feels it is appropriate.

See Chapter 1 Section 2.10 of your CISI Workbook

50. **B** Warning Notices, Decision Notices and Further Decision Notices are referred to as being statutory notices.

See Chapter 1 Section 2.10.1 of your CISI Workbook

51. **B** The FCA may publish a warning notice regarding disciplinary action proposed against an individual but only after the recipient has been consulted.

See Chapter 1 Section 1.2.2 of your CISI Workbook

52. **B** Members of Lloyd's are exempt persons, but the institution of Lloyd's is not exempt and, thus, requires authorisation from the FCA.

See Chapter 1 Section 1.7 of your CISI Workbook

53. **C** It is the Financial Conduct Authority that grants Approved Person status to employees undertaking a controlled function.

See Chapter 1 Section 1.7.1 of your CISI Workbook

54. **C** A Notice of Discontinuance (s 389 FSMA 2000) must be issued where proceedings set out in a Decision or Warning Notice are being discontinued.

See Chapter 1 Section 2.10.1 of your CISI Workbook

55. **C** National Savings and Investments products are not specified investments under FSMA 2000. The fact the deposit account is tax-exempt is irrelevant to its status as a specified investment.

See Chapter 1 Section 1.3.4 of your CISI Workbook

56. **A** Arranging deals in investments would have been a regulated activity. However, forex trades are not specified investments.

See Chapter 1 Section 1.5 of your CISI Workbook

57. **C** Although refusing to attend a meeting would be an offence, it is possible that failure could be justified (eg illness).

See Chapter 1 Section 2.9 of your CISI Workbook

58. **B** Section 165 of FSMA states information must be provided within a reasonable period.

See Chapter 1 Section 2.9 of your CISI Workbook

59. **C** Part 4A permission gives authorisation for the UK only. The activity may be passportable under EU Directives such as MiFID to other EEA countries but only in relation to MiFID or other relevant business.

See Chapter 1 Section 1.3.1 of your CISI Workbook

60. **D** A publisher's Tip Sheet is an example of an excluded activity and, therefore, is not exempt. The other three are all exempt from the requirement to be authorised.

See Chapter 1 Section 1.6.2 of your CISI Workbook

61. **B** Principle 7: communications with clients must be 'clear, fair and not misleading'.

See Chapter 1 Section 2.2 of your CISI Workbook

62. **D** Only the **first four** Statements of Principle apply to **all** approved persons. The final three only apply to those doing a significant influence function.

See Chapter 1 Section 2.3.1 of your CISI Workbook

63. **A** Information for clients is not one of the principles. It is valuable to remember the principles, as they are commonly tested.

See Chapter 1 Section 2.2 of your CISI Workbook

64. **D** Client assets is the correct principle rather than customer assets.

See Chapter 1 Section 2.2 of your CISI Workbook

65. **A** The question refers to the Statements of Principles for individuals, four of which apply to all approved persons and three of which apply to significant influence functions only. There are 16 controlled functions and 11 Principles for Businesses.

See Chapter 1 Section 2.3 of your CISI Workbook

66. **C** Records of senior management changes must be recorded for six years from the date of change The other record-keeping rule is for anti-money laundering rules where records must be kept for five years. Memory aid: six letters in 'senior' and five letters in 'money' and 'MiFID'.

See Chapter 1 Section 2.5.2 of your CISI Workbook

67. **C** The false item has deliberately confused Principle 4: Financial Prudence and Principle 5: Market Conduct.

See Chapter 1 Section 2.2 of your CISI Workbook

68. **D** The Principles for Business are known by their number.

See Chapter 1 Section 2.2 of your CISI Workbook

69. **B** Independence would be otherwise addressed through Principles 1 and 3, but it is not explicitly addressed as a statement of principle.

See Chapter 1 Section 2.3.1 of your CISI Workbook

70. **C** Although answer D is also correct as the **maximum** penalty is both prison **and** the fine, answer C is the best answer as it correctly describes the fact that imprisonment and fines are 'and/or'.

See Chapter 1 Section 1.3 of your CISI Workbook

71. **B** Futures contracts are investments if bought for investment purposes, but not if bought for commercial purposes.

See Chapter 1 Section 1.3.4 of your CISI Workbook

72. **B** The passporting process is under the Market in Financial Instruments Directive, and only those firms conducting activities specified in the Directive may passport those activities.

See Chapter 1 Section 8.2.1 of your CISI Workbook

73. **D** Euroclear (UK and Ireland) is a Recognised Clearing House (RCH).

See Chapter 1 Section 1.2.8 of your CISI Workbook

74. **C** Conducting unauthorised investment business is a breach of the Financial Services and Markets Act 2000. Section 19 of FSMA 2000 states that a firm must be authorised.

See Chapter 1 Section 1.3 of your CISI Workbook

75. **D** The publication of the Tip Sheet by media would be excluded, not the advice on it.

See Chapter 1 Section 1.6.2 of your CISI Workbook

76. **A** The Tokyo Stock Exchange is a Designated Investment Exchange. As it does not do any activities in or into the UK, it does not require exemption from UK law.

See Chapter 1 Sections 1.2.6 and 1.2.7 of your CISI Workbook

77. **B** NYSE as a DIE does not need exemption from UK law as it does not operate in or into the UK.

See Chapter 1 Sections 1.2.6 and 1.2.7 of your CISI Workbook

78. **B** A Prohibition Order is issued under s 56 of FSMA against a person to prohibit them doing anything in relation to financial services in the UK. As such the prohibited person will NOT be an approved person under the FCA regime and therefore not subject to its disciplinary powers.

See Chapter 1 Section 2.10.5 of your CISI Workbook

79. **C** Carefully read the question to note that it specifies EXEMPT persons, not excluded. Media (newspapers, TV and radio) and unremunerated trustees are excluded, not exempt. As a memory technique it may help to remember that excluded activities are those when there was no intention to regulate these people, they were unintentionally caught in the definition. Exempt persons are doing regulated activities, but they are regulated in another way than through FCA authorisation. In this case, lawyers, actuaries and accountants have their own professional regulators.

See Chapter 1 Section 1.7 of your CISI Workbook

80. **B** The FCA has extensive sanctions available to it. It may seek injunctions and restitution orders, impose fines, remove the approved person status of an individual, vary or cancel permissions, suspend the approval or ban a person from working in the authorised sector.

See Chapter 1 Section 2.10.3 of your CISI Workbook

81. **B** Unit trusts, in which there is no secondary market, are excluded from the legislation.

See Chapter 1 Section 5.2.1 of your CISI Workbook

82. **D** Insider dealing only relates to securities and derivatives on securities, whereas market abuse can occur in relation to commodity derivatives trading on a prescribed market.

See Chapter 1 Section 5.2.1 of your CISI Workbook

83. **D** The legislation on market abuse is found the EU MAR.

See Chapter 1 Section 7.1 of your CISI Workbook

84. **A** Minimising your tax liability through 'tax avoidance' is not a criminal activity.

See Chapter 1 Section 4.1 of your CISI Workbook

85. **C** Going to the police should not be necessary at this stage.

See Chapter 1 Section 4.3.4 of your CISI Workbook

86. **A** The guidance notes are just that – there for guidance. The JMLSG is not part of the FCA.

See Chapter 1 Section 4.3.4 of your CISI Workbook

87. **B** Criminal Justice Act 1993 covers trading in shares, debt securities issued by the private or public sector, warrants, depository receipts, options, futures or Contracts for Difference (CFDs) on any of the foregoing.

See Chapter 1 Section 5.2.1 of your CISI Workbook

88. **C** **All** employees, by virtue of their office, are potential holders of inside information.

See Chapter 1 Section 5.1 of your CISI Workbook

89. **D** Controlled functions relate to the approved person regime, which is being replaced by the Accountability Regime.

See Chapter 1 Section 2.6.1 of your CISI Workbook

90. **C** The three stages in the money laundering process are placement, layering and integration. The criminal activity to get the funds in the first place is not included.

See Chapter 1 Section 4.1 of your CISI Workbook

91. **C** Disclosing inside information can be prosecuted even if trading has not occurred.

See Chapter 1 Section 5.2 of your CISI Workbook

92. **C** The maximum would be a prison sentence together with a fine. Remember, liability does not require money laundering to have happened; simply not having the appropriate procedures in place is deemed bad enough.

See Chapter 1 Section 4.3 of your CISI Workbook

93. **D** The fine is unlimited. As market abuse is a **civil** offence, there is no jail sentence available. As an FCA rule would have been broken, an approved person could face FCA disciplinary action.

See Chapter 1 Section 7.1 of your CISI Workbook

94. **D** Insider dealing legislation covers equity and debt and related products, such as depository receipts, warrants, derivatives, contracts for differences and all tradable debt instruments but not collective investment schemes, life insurance policies or commodities such as currency or gold. The index future may be relevant if used with other products to create an exposure to a specific security. An investor does not determine the investment policy of a fund and so cannot be sure it invests in the specific security on which inside information is held.

See Chapter 1 Section 5.2.1 of your CISI Workbook

95. **C** Had the question asked about the maximum penalty in the Crown Court the answer would be seven years and an unlimited fine.

See Chapter 1 Section 5.2.2 of your CISI Workbook

96. **A** A hostile takeover is not in itself abusive.

See Chapter 1 Section 7.1 of your CISI Workbook

97. **C** Whilst the MLRO must also report suspicions to NCA, this question concerns **your** suspicions as an employee.

See Chapter 1 Section 4.4.1 of your CISI Workbook

98. **C** The FCA can ask the court to impose an injunction, restitution or other penalty. Fines can be unlimited.

See Chapter 1 Section 7.1 of your CISI Workbook

99. **C** Processing proceeds of crime relates to money laundering.

See Chapter 1 Section 7.2 of your CISI Workbook

100. **D** The regular market user test is part of the civil offence of market abuse, not the criminal offence of insider dealing.

See Chapter 1 Section 7.5 of your CISI Workbook

101. **D** Remember that money laundering regulations require retention of records for five years.

See Chapter 1 Section 4.3.4 of your CISI Workbook

102. **B** Insider dealing legislation relates to the securities of companies (ie bonds and shares) and thus excludes foreign currencies.

See Chapter 1 Section 5.2.1 of your CISI Workbook

103. **A**   Money laundering is a criminal offence.

See Chapter 1 Section 4.1 of your CISI Workbook

104. **D**   Insider dealing is a criminal offence whereas behaviour based on information that is not generally available would be a civil offence under the market abuse regime.

See Chapter 1 Section 7.1 of your CISI Workbook

105. **A**   This would be for the offence of assistance (or arrangements).

See Chapter 1 Section 4.2.1 of your CISI Workbook

106. **B**   Only a court order may be used to sequester funds.

See Chapter 1 Section 5.2.2 of your CISI Workbook

107. **D**   Part V of the Criminal Justice Act 1993 provides the insider dealing legislation.

See Chapter 1 Section 5.1 of your CISI Workbook

108. **D**   This is the process by which money from illegal sources are made to appear legally derived.

See Chapter 1 Section 4.1 of your CISI Workbook

109. **D**   NCA stands for National Crime Agency (formerly Serious Organised Crime Agency SOCA). This is the organisation which reviews all money laundering suspicion reports generated by the financial industry.

See Chapter 1 Section 4.4.1 of your CISI Workbook

110. **D**   In this case, the shares index is not specific enough to use the inside information whereas the other three are specific ownership of a security.

See Chapter 1 Section 4.1 of your CISI Workbook

111. **A**   The Code of Market Conduct is written by the FCA and is found in the FCA Handbook. It contains guidance not legislation.

See Chapter 1 Section 7.6 of your CISI Workbook

112. **D**   Seven years imprisonment and statutory fine. As a memory technique it is easy to remember that the word 'insider' has seven letters: thus seven years imprisonment. The statutory fine, as specified in the Criminal Justice Act, is unlimited.

See Chapter 1 Section 5.2 of your CISI Workbook

113. **C**   A breach of the criminal offence of misleading statements and impressions carries a maximum penalty of seven years imprisonment and an unlimited fine.

See Chapter 1 Section 6.1 of your CISI Workbook

114. **A** The Proceeds of Crime Act applies to actions by individuals and provides that the maximum penalty for assisting a money launderer is 14 years' imprisonment and an unlimited fine. As a memory technique it is easy to remember that for the offence of assisting a money launderer we **double** the penalty of the other two main financial crimes (insider dealing and misleading statements) – and that there are 14 letters in 'money launderer'.

See Chapter 1 Section 4.2 of your CISI Workbook

115. **B** A money launderer will first need to **place** the illegal proceeds into the financial system; then **layer** it with proceeds from a clean source in order to separate the proceeds of crime from their original offence; and finally, **integrate** the proceeds back into the mainstream financial sector where they will appear legal.

See Chapter 1 Section 4.1 of your CISI Workbook

116. **D** The maximum Crown Court penalty is ten years' imprisonment plus an unlimited fine.

See Chapter 1 Section 4.6 of your CISI Workbook

117. **D** The Bribery Act has a wide ranging territorial scope and offences committed outside the UK by UK citizens are covered by the legislation.

See Chapter 1 Section 4.6 of your CISI Workbook

118. **B** A private company must give a minimum of 14 days' notice of a general meeting.

See Chapter 1 Section 3.6.1 of your CISI Workbook

119. **C** Twenty-one days' notice is required for a public company AGM.

See Chapter 1 Section 3.6.1 of your CISI Workbook

120. **A** Directors would normally call an GM, however members holding at least 5% of the voting shares may requisition that the directors call a GM (for both private and public companies.

See Chapter 1 Section 3.6.2 of your CISI Workbook

121. **A** In general, a 'quorum' is achieved when two members (or their proxies) are present.

See Chapter 1 Section 3.6.4 of your CISI Workbook

122. **A** All general meetings require 21 calendar days' notice, unless a resolution is passed to shorten this.

See Chapter 1 Section 3.6.1 of your CISI Workbook

123. **A** Section 793 gives a public company the power to require shareholders to give information. The company secretary is responsible for dealing with the requirements of a s 793 Notice.

See Chapter 1 Section 3.7 of your CISI Workbook

124. **C** Waiving of notice for a GM would require 95% of shareholders to consent.

See Chapter 1 Section 3.6.1 of your CISI Workbook

125. **B**   Approving significant capital expenditures will be done at the Board Meeting of Directors.

See Chapter 1 Section 3.6 of your CISI Workbook

126. **A**   If a private company offers shares to the public the company and its directors may be subject to unlimited fines.

See Chapter 1 Section 3.8.2 of your CISI Workbook

127. **A**   Issued share capital would not be included in the Articles, it would be found in the company's balance sheet, shown within shareholders' funds.

See Chapter 1 Section 3.8.1 of your CISI Workbook

128. **C**   There is no restriction on shareholders buying further shares with dividends they receive. An indemnity would mean the company agreeing to buy the shares from an investor if the price fell below a certain level, thus offering financial assistance for the purchase of the company's own shares.

See Chapter 1 Section 3.5 of your CISI Workbook

FCA Conduct of Business Sourcebook

Questions

1. **Which of the following would be a per se professional client in relation to non-MiFID business?**

   A   A company with net assets of £2m

   B   A partnership with net assets of £4m

   C   A public authority

   D   A trust with assets of £3m

2. **Which of the following is not true of Chinese walls?**

   A   They are artificial barriers to the flow of information

   B   They can exist between different subsidiaries of the same group

   C   They are required when a part of the firm is doing regulated activities

   D   When a Chinese wall is in place, a firm will not be found guilty of market abuse due to its actions

3. **What is the best description of a Chinese wall?**

   A   It is permitted as an alternative to the Personal Account Notice

   B   A firm must have it to prevent conflicts of interest

   C   It is used to prevent employees talking to each other

   D   It is used to prevent the flow of information between departments

4. **The COBS sourcebook applies to all of the following, except:**

   A   Motor insurance

   B   Designated investment business

   C   Long-term life assurance

   D   Accepting deposits

5. **All of the following are allowable ways of managing a conflict of interest, except:**

   A   Procedures designed to restrict the flow of confidential information

   B   A conflicts of interest policy

   C   Disclosure of the conflict to the Financial Conduct Authority

   D   Establishing a Chinese wall

6.   **Which of the following statements concerning Chinese walls is true?**

A   Firms are not required to have Chinese walls in place

B   The FCA rules specify how they must be structured

C   They only involve physical segregation

D   They are external arrangements

7.   **Which of the following best describes the application of COBS rules with regard to a UK firm dealing in bonds with an eligible counterparty?**

A   As a fully regulated activity, all the Conduct of Business rules

B   As inter-professional business, the inter-professional conduct rules apply

C   COBS rule apply as appropriate, given the domicile of the counterparty

D   Limited COBS protections apply

8.   **The Conduct of Business rules detail:**

A   Management of control risks

B   Regulated activities and specified investment

C   The statutory objectives of the FCA

D   The requirements controlling the behaviour of firms

9.   **All of the following could be classified as a 'per se' eligible counterparty, except:**

A   An inter-dealer broker

B   A broker-dealer

C   A central bank

D   A large undertaking that has given express consent

10. **Which of the following would need to elect to be an eligible counterparty?**

A   Another FCA authorised firm

B   A central bank

C   A local authority

D   A UCITS collective investment scheme manager

11. **Which of the following is most accurate regarding the COBS rules on inducements?**

A   The rules only apply to all dealings with retail clients

B   The rules apply for dealings with retail clients and professional clients

C   The rules apply for dealings with all categories of client

D   The rules apply only when undertaking MiFID business with all categories of client

12. **Under the COBS rule of reliance on others, a firm may rely on information provided by all of the following, except:**

   A   An unconnected authorised person

   B   A professional firm

   C   A person connected to the firm

   D   An expert competent person

13. **According to Principle 8, when conflicts of interest arise, an authorised firm should:**

   A   Manage them fairly

   B   Decline to act

   C   Suspend the Chinese wall for that transaction

   D   Keep a record of the conflict

14. **The rules for unwritten promotions include all of the following, except:**

   A   They may only be made at an appropriate time of day

   B   The investor should understand the purpose of the call

   C   The call should be terminated immediately if the investor makes it clear that they do not wish the call to continue

   D   A draft client agreement should be sent to a retail client immediately after the call

15. **Which of the following is most accurate regarding the approval of financial promotions for overseas firms by a UK authorised firm?**

   A   UK firms must not approve any financial promotions for overseas firms

   B   UK firms may approve financial promotions by any overseas firms following the same rules it would if the firm were UK based

   C   UK firms may approve financial promotions for overseas firms if they explain the investor protection rules which will not apply and the extent to which UK compensation schemes will be available

   D   UK firms may approve financial promotions for overseas firms if they agree to fully underwrite any potential loss suffered by UK clients

16. **Which one of the following would make a company a professional client in relation to non-MiFID business?**

   A   More than 20 members and net assets or share capital of £500,000 or more

   B   Share capital of £5m or more

   C   Cash plus investments of £10m or more

   D   More than 20 members

17. **Which of the following is true in relation to Chinese walls?**

A   Firms are always required to have Chinese walls

B   Firms are never required to have Chinese walls

C   Firms are only required to have Chinese walls if they are of sufficient size to justify them

D   Firms are only required to have Chinese walls if they are carrying out regulated or ancillary activities

18. **What is the best description of a Chinese wall?**

A   Physical barrier

B   It must involve a policy of independence

C   All firms with more than one division must have them

D   Arrangements to prevent the flow of information

19. **The Personal Account Dealing Rules would apply to:**

A   All employees

B   Employees for sole trading firms

C   Relevant persons whose activities might lead to conflicts of interest

D   All approved persons

20. **Which of the following is NOT a permitted unsolicited real-time financial promotion (cold call)?**

A   An unsolicited call to a retail client regarding a Regulated Investment Scheme which is not a high volatility fund

B   An unsolicited call to a retail client regarding a Life Assurance Policy linked to a high volatility fund

C   An unsolicited call to a retail client regarding an Authorised Unit Trust ISA not linked to a high volatility fund

D   A call to an individual where an existing client relationship exists and where the nature and type of product discussed is envisaged

21. **The rule on prohibiting inducements under COBS in relation to MiFID business personal recommendations applies to all of the following, except:**

A   Paid commissions

B   Shared commissions

C   Contingent commissions

D   Disclosable commissions

22. **All of the following are normally covered by Financial Promotions Order exemptions, except:**

    A Communications only to investment professionals

    B Communications to a company's creditors

    C Communications by the Bank of England

    D Communications on the internet

23. **The regulator's Financial Promotions rules cover:**

    I A financial promotion within the UK

    II An unwritten cold call from the UK aimed at non-UK investors

    III Issuance and approval of financial promotions within the UK

    IV An incoming promotion from an EEA firm in respect of MiFID business

    A I, II, III and IV

    B II, III and IV only

    C I and III only

    D I, II and III only

24. **Which pair of words most accurately describes a 'financial promotion'?**

    A Advertisement/encouragement

    B Incentive/publicity

    C Invitation/inducement

    D Prospectus/upgrade

25. **Which type of information is not normally needed when assessing the suitability of a client?**

    A Knowledge and experience

    B Financial situation

    C Investment objectives

    D Age and proximity to retirement

26. **Under MiFID, one of the conditions that a retail client needs to satisfy in order to become an elective professional client is to pass a 'quantitative' test. This test consists of satisfying two requirements out of a possible three. Which of the following tests is not one of the three options?**

    A The client has traded, in significant size, on the relevant market at an average frequency of ten transactions per quarter over the previous four quarters

    B The client's portfolio exceeds €500,000

    C The client works/has worked in financial sector for at least one year in a professional position which requires knowledge of transactions/services

    D If the client is a UK-based private person they must have passed an examination of the Chartered Institute for Securities and Investment

27. **An employee of an authorised firm wants to trade for themselves. Which of these statements is most correct?**

   A   The employee must trade through an account with their firm

   B   The employee must notify the Money Laundering Reporting Officer of all trades that they do

   C   The employee does not have to use an account at their firm but there must be a system to enable trades to be reported to their firm

   D   The employee must hold all investments for a minimum of six weeks and is not allowed to trade shares in their own company

28. **Which one of the following can be classified as a per se professional client of a MiFID firm?**

   A   A company with net assets of €12.5m and net turnover of €20m

   B   A company with €10m balance sheet total and €32m net turnover

   C   The manager of a regulated collective investment scheme

   D   A large business with €20m funds to invest

29. **The personal account dealing policy will aim to prevent employees from:**

   A   Dealing in equity issued by their firm after the Board of Directors made an announcement about the profits

   B   Dealing on the basis of information contained in draft research reports

   C   Dealing in securities held on the own account of the firm

   D   Dealing on exchanges that are not given the status of a recognised investment exchange

30. **The rule on inducements:**

   A   Prevents authorised firms from making and receiving payments which can lead to avoidance of their duty to the client

   B   Prohibits the firm to receive any payments from third party providers

   C   Requires detailed disclosure of all inducements received

   D   Protects the interests of retail clients only

31. **A direct offer financial promotion might be best described as an offer to:**

   A   Enter into an agreement with a high net worth individual without receiving further information

   B   Discuss an agreement with a new potential customer without receiving further information

   C   Investors to purchase investments directly 'off-the-page' without receiving further information

   D   Extend an agreement with an existing customer without receiving further information

32. **Which of the following statements about rules governing investment research activities is the least correct?**

A Financial analysts can take positions in securities contrary to their current recommendations only in exceptional circumstances and with senior permission

B Analysts must refrain from dealing on the information contained in research until the clients have been provided with time to consider it

C Research analysts must not promise issuers favourable research coverage

D The issuer should be permitted to review unpublished research on their company at any time

33. **The largest client of Van Leuven Investments is Jump plc, with whom the firm carries on non-MiFID business. Jump plc has a balance sheet total of €15,000,000 and 150 full-time employees. Last year, Jump plc had a turnover of €20,000,000. Based on the information available, what would be the most appropriate client categorisation for Jump plc?**

A Private client

B Retail client

C Per se professional client

D Per se eligible counterparty

34. **Barlow & Barlow (B&B) is a firm of financial advisers offering services to a wide variety of clients including large firms, investment banks and small individual private investors. The firm specialises in providing research and advice into specialist areas including the pharmaceutical sector, but also offer more general financial advice.**

Patrick is a retail client of B&B with a portfolio worth £450,000 who requests in writing that he be treated as an elective professional client with respect to share purchases. This will be MiFID business. Patrick has worked for a major bank for nine months carrying out daily transactions in equity dealing.

B&B should treat Patrick:

A As a retail client for the reason that he does not satisfy the quantitative test for MiFID business

B As a retail client for the reason that he does not satisfy the qualitative test

C As a per se professional client

D As an elective professional client

35. **When a firm provides performance information in relation to MiFID business, what is the period to which it must relate?**

A At least the three preceding years or the whole period of the life of the product if this is less than five years

B At least the five preceding years, but if the product has been established for less than five years, then only three years data need be used

C At least the five preceding years or the whole period of the life of the product if this is less than five years

D The preceding 12 months

36. **Under MiFID, if an investment firm sets up a branch in another EEA state, to whose local rules must the branch adhere?**

   A   Home state

   B   Host state

   C   Home and host states

   D   Home or host state (the branch can choose which rules to follow)

37. **Which of the following is not a client category under MiFID?**

   A   Professional client

   B   Eligible counterparty

   C   Retail client

   D   Intermediate client

38. **Which two of the following tests indicate whether a firm should treat a client as an elective professional client?**

   A   Qualitative test and mandatory test

   B   Mandatory test and quantitative test

   C   Qualitative test and quantitative test

   D   Mandatory test and management test

39. **An employee of a firm carrying out designated investment business with a client enters into a trade with an eligible counterparty using her own money. Which of the following best describes what she should do?**

   A   Report the trade to the regulator's Market Supervision Department

   B   Inform HM Treasury

   C   Inform HMRC

   D   Follow the firm's policy on personal account dealing

40. **What persons are protected by the best execution rules?**

   A   Clients generally

   B   Retail clients generally

   C   Retail and professional clients generally

   D   Retail and professional clients, but professional clients can opt out

41. **With respect to 'best execution criteria', which of the following characteristics does a firm not have to take into account?**

   A   The client's categorisation

   B   The financial instruments

   C   The previous day's closing price

   D   The execution venues

42. **Which need not be included in a direct offer financial promotion?**

A   List of execution venues

B   Nature of services provided

C   Charges and remuneration

D   Arrangements for holding client assets

43. **Which of the following is not a per se eligible counterparty?**

A   Insurance company

B   Pension fund

C   Central bank

D   Treasury department of a large oil company

44. **You hear a colleague mentioning the term 'common platform'. This term describes:**

A   The trading platform provided by a Multilateral Trading Facility (MTF)

B   The set of governance principles laid out in the UK Corporate Governance Code

C   A unified set of organisational and systems and controls requirements applying to firms that are subject to the Capital Requirements Directive and/or MiFID

D   The requirements applying to all investment advisers from 31 December 2012 that result from the Retail Distribution Review

Answers

1.　**C**　A large undertaking needs assets of at least £5m to be a professional client in relation to non-MiFID business. Local and public authorities are per se professional clients for non-MiFID business, however, they would be classed as a retail client for MiFID business.

See Chapter 2 Section 4.1.3 of your CISI Workbook

2.　**C**　They are a possible way of ensuring that other parts of a firm do not have a conflict of interest with another part of the firm, but they are not compulsory.

See Chapter 2 Section 5.5 of your CISI Workbook

3.　**D**　Chinese walls are not compulsory, they are just one of the ways a firm may manage its conflict of interest.

See Chapter 2 Section 5.5 of your CISI Workbook

4.　**A**　COBS only applies to long-term insurance such as life policies as they have an investment element. It does not apply to short-term insurance such as car and home insurance.

See Chapter 2 Section 1.1 of your CISI Workbook

5.　**C**　The disclosure of the potential conflict is made to the clients, not the FCA.

See Chapter 2 Section 5 of your CISI Workbook

6.　**A**　Chinese walls are **internal** arrangements designed to prevent the flow of confidential information that often involve physical segregation of persons but may also be technological barriers. The FCA rules allow the use of Chinese walls but do not set out how to structure them.

See Chapter 2 Section 5.5 of your CISI Workbook

7.　**D**　Trades between eligible counterparties are covered by the conduct of business rules that apply to all clients, such as the client classification rules.

See Chapter 2 Section 1.1.1 of your CISI Workbook

8.　**D**　A, B and C are covered by other aspects of FSMA 2000 or the FCA Handbook.

See Chapter 2 Section 1.1 of your CISI Workbook

9.　**D**　IDBs and broker-dealers will be financial institutions and therefore per se eligible counterparties (ECPs) in relation to MiFID business. A large undertaking consenting to be treated as an ECP is known as an 'elective' rather than 'per se' ECP.

See Chapter 2 Section 4.1.3 of your CISI Workbook

10.　**C**　A local authority has the right to opt up to eligible counterparty status; the others are 'per se' eligible counterparties.

See Chapter 2 Section 4.2.3 of your CISI Workbook

11. **B**   The COBS inducement rules apply when undertaking both MiFID and non MiFID business with professional and retail clients.

See Chapter 2 Section 2.2 of your CISI Workbook

12. **C**   The provider must be competent (ie FCA authorised or professional, eg a lawyer) and unconnected.

See Chapter 2 Section 2.3 of your CISI Workbook

13. **A**   Principle 8 requires that when conflicts arise, the firm manages the conflict to ensure that customers are treated fairly. The SYSC rules then specify a number of methods to achieve this.

See Chapter 2 Section 5.1 and chapter 1 Section 2.2 of your CISI Workbook

14. **D**   This is not a requirement of the financial promotions rules.

See Chapter 2 Section 3.2.4 of your CISI Workbook

15. **C**   The firm may also choose to describe any overseas protection schemes that are in place. They must have no doubts that the overseas firm will behave honestly and reliably with UK clients.

See Chapter 2 Section 3.2.4 of your CISI Workbook

16. **B**   The number of members is only relevant for pension funds for client classification.

See Chapter 2 Section 4.1.3 of your CISI Workbook

17. **B**   Firms are never obliged to use Chinese walls. They are just one possible method of making sure a firm meets its obligations to manage a conflict of interest.

See Chapter 2 Section 5.5 of your CISI Workbook

18. **D**   For reference, there is never any obligation to have these Chinese walls.

See Chapter 2 Section 5.5 of your CISI Workbook

19. **C**   Personal account dealing rules apply to all relevant persons who have involvement with activities that might lead to conflicts of interest (or who have access to confidential or inside information).

See Chapter 2 Section 6 of your CISI Workbook

20. **B**   An unsolicited financial promotion (cold call) is one which the client has not expressly requested. A client may be called regarding any marketable packaged product (excluding higher volatility funds) and controlled activities concerning readily realisable investments (excluding warrants). A cold call regarding a life policy linked to a high volatility fund would not be allowable. Calls to an individual where an existing client relationship exists and where the nature and type of product discussed is envisaged are allowable.

See Chapter 2 Section 3.2.4 of your CISI Workbook

21. **D**   As disclosure is required, the inducement rule protections are not as necessary.

See Chapter 2 Section 2.2 of your CISI Workbook

22. **D** Internet sales are covered by the financial promotions rules.

See Chapter 2 Section 3.1.5 of your CISI Workbook

23. **D** Unwritten cold calls made to persons outside of the UK still require the firm to follow regulatory rules. The incoming promotion would be considered cross border business and covered by the rules of the firm's home state.

See Chapter 2 Section 3.2.1 of your CISI Workbook

24. **C** The words 'invitation' and 'inducement' are those used in the regulator's description.

See Chapter 2 Section 3.1.1 of your CISI Workbook

25. **D** It is possible that age and proximity to retirement may arise during the assessment but they are not deemed to be necessary information.

See Chapter 2 Section 7.2.1 of your CISI Workbook

26. **D** The quantitative test does not include a requirement for clients to pass CISI exams!

See Chapter 2 Section 4.2.2 of your CISI Workbook

27. **C** Firms must keep records of all personal transactions notified by them and of any authorisation or prohibition made in connection with them. Employees do not have to use an account at their firm but there must be a system to enable trades to be reported to the employees' firm.

See Chapter 2 Section 6.2 of your CISI Workbook

28. **C** The 20/40/2 rule for large undertakings is not satisfied in any of the examples; the fund manager is an authorised firm and therefore is by default a professional client.

See Chapter 2 Section 4.1.3 of your CISI Workbook

29. **B** Dealing ahead of publication of reports is prohibited as this puts the recipient of the research at a disadvantage in comparison to the employee of the firm.

See Chapter 2 Section 6.1 of your CISI Workbook

30. **A** The rule on inducements protects the interests of all clients. Only summary disclosure of fees/commissions/non-monetary benefits from third party providers are required. Detailed disclosure must be provided on request.

See Chapter 2 Section 2.2 of your CISI Workbook

31. **C** A direct offer financial promotion must contain appropriate disclosures and for non-MiFID business additional information so that the client is reasonably able to understand the risks and make investment decisions on an informed basis.

See Chapter 2 Section 3.2.3 of your CISI Workbook

32. **D** Pre-publication drafts can be previewed by the issuer only for the purpose of verifying compliance.

See Chapter 2 Section 5.6 of your CISI Workbook

33.　**B**　The quantitative test for professional clients when carrying out non-MiFID business requires two of the following:

€12,500,000 balance sheet total

€25,000,000 net turnover

250 average number of employees in the year

Thus, the company would not be treated as a per se professional client and would be treated as a retail client.

See Chapter 2 Section 4.2.2 of your CISI Workbook

34.　**A**　While it is likely that the client satisfies the qualitative test, we are unable to show that he satisfies two of the criteria for the quantitative test, which are:

- The client has carried out at least ten 'significant' transactions per quarter on the relevant market, over the last four quarters

- The client's portfolio, including cash deposits, exceeds €500,000

- The client has knowledge of the transactions envisaged from at least one year's professional work in the financial sector

B&B should therefore treat Patrick as a retail client.

See Chapter 2 Section 4.2.2 of your CISI Workbook

35.　**C**　At least the five preceding years or the whole period of the life of the product if this is less than five years – this is the correct answer.

See Chapter 2 Section 3.2.2 of your CISI Workbook

36.　**C**　If a firm has a physical presence in another EEA country, it must adhere to the local rules of that country for most of the Conduct of Business rules. However, there are a few minor exceptions, such as personal account dealing rules, that follow the home state rules.

See Chapter 2 Section 1.1.2 of your CISI Workbook

37.　**D**　'Intermediate client' is not currently a client category.

See Chapter 2 Section 4.1.3 of your CISI Workbook

38.　**C**　'Mandatory test' and 'management test' are invented terms. The qualitative test requires experience, expertise and knowledge. The quantitative test requires a certain frequency of transactions, minimum portfolio value and/or knowledge of transactions from professional work in the financial sector.

See Chapter 2 Section 4.2.2 of your CISI Workbook

39.　**D**　The regulator requires authorised firms to develop a personal account dealing policy and make employees aware of it. The specific actions of the employee will be detailed in that policy.

See Chapter 2 Section 6.2 of your CISI Workbook

40.   **C**   The best execution rule is aimed at protecting both retail and professional clients. Professional clients cannot opt out of best execution. The term 'clients generally' would include eligible counterparties.

See Chapter 2 Section 7.3 of your CISI Workbook

41.   **C**   Prices can move dramatically from one day to another and so, when seeking 'best execution' today, yesterday's price is not relevant.

See Chapter 2 Section 7.3 of your CISI Workbook

42.   **A**   A direct offer financial promotion must contain any necessary disclosures relevant to that offer or invitation, eg information about the firm and its services, information about costs and associated charges, a description of the nature and risks of the designated investment and information regarding safeguarding assets and client money.

See Chapter 2 Section 3.2.3 of your CISI Workbook

43.   **D**   All the others are included in the list of per se eligible counterparties. A large oil company is simply a large company and is not included.

See Chapter 2 Section 4.1.3 of your CISI Workbook

44.   **C**   Certain principles and rules apply to 'common platform' firms, which comprise firms that are subject to either or both of MiFID and CRD.

See Chapter 2 Section 5.2 of your CISI Workbook

Corporate Governance and Business Ethics

Questions

1. **Which of the following best complies with the principles of corporate governance?**

    A   Directors' remuneration should have a performance related element

    B   Directors should be allotted share options

    C   Executive directors may set executive remuneration if it is subject to shareholder approval

    D   Details of executive remuneration should be contained in the audit report

2. **Which of the following is consistent with the principles of corporate governance?**

    A   Directors should report on the company's progress to shareholders

    B   Directors are ultimately accountable to the Chief Executive

    C   Non-executive directors are made up of the representatives of institutional shareholders

    D   Executive directors set executive remuneration

3. **The UK Corporate Governance Code can best be described as:**

    A   A statutory code introduced under FSMA 2000

    B   A non-statutory code of best practice enforced through FCA rules

    C   A statutory code enforced through MiFID

    D   A non-statutory code enforced by HM Treasury

4. **The UK Corporate Governance Code deals with all of the following, except:**

    A   Relations with shareholders

    B   Relations with institutional shareholders

    C   Relations with regulators

    D   Accountability of directors

5. **Which one of the following type of directorship is encouraged under the UK Corporate Governance Code?**

    A   Executive directors

    B   Impartial directors

    C   Non-executive directors

    D   Active directors

6. **Which piece of legislation enforces the UK Corporate Governance Code?**

    A   Corporate Governance Act 2002

    B   Financial Services and Markets Act 2000

    C   Directors' Responsibilities Act 1999

    D   None, as it is non-statutory

7. Don Smith, employed by Hunter Investment Advice Limited, provides investment advice to the board of trustees of a private university endowment fund. The trustees have given Smith the fund's financial information, including planned expenditures. Smith received a phone call on Friday afternoon from Mark Murdock, a prominent alumnus, requesting that Smith fax to him comprehensive financial information about the fund. According to Murdock, he has a potential contributor but needs the information today to close the deal and cannot contact any of the trustees. Based on business ethics, Smith may:

   A Send Murdock the information because disclosure would benefit the client

   B Send Murdock the information provided Smith promptly notifies the trustees

   C Send Murdock the information because it is not material non-public information

   D Not send Murdock the information because Smith must preserve confidentiality

8. Which one of the following is not part of the UK Corporate Governance Code?

   A One-third of the board of a FTSE 350 company should consist of independent non-executive directors

   B The same individual should not carry out the role of both the Chairman and Chief Executive

   C Executives should not hold more than one additional non-executive position with other companies

   D Non-executive director remuneration should reflect the complexity of the responsibilities

9. To whom does the CISI Code of Conduct apply?

   A All authorised firms

   B All approved persons

   C All CISI members

   D All employees of authorised firms

10. Which one of the following best describes the purpose of the UK Corporate Governance Code?

    A To set out best practice on takeovers and mergers

    B To improve shareholder democracy in UK companies

    C To promote best practice in the performance of the duties of directors of UK companies

    D To improve transparency in directors' share dealings in their own companies

11. Which of the following is not a disciplinary matter for the FCA?

    A Breach of a Conduct of Business Rule

    B Breach of the CISI Code of Conduct

    C Failure to observe a Warning Notice

    D Failure to observe a Decision Notice

Answers

1. **A**   Non-executive directors set executive pay, which should be linked to performance either using a share based incentive plan, share options or other appropriate means. The details must be set out in the report of the remuneration committee not the audit report.

    See Chapter 3 Section 1.2.4 of your CISI Workbook

2. **A**   Directors are accountable to shareholders and must report on the company's progress to shareholders in the Annual Report and at the AGM. Non-executive directors should be independent and not drawn from the major suppliers or shareholders of the company, or be former employees.

    See Chapter 3 Section 1.2.5 of your CISI Workbook

3. **B**   There is no legislation behind the UK Corporate Governance Code, but it does have the backing of the FCA Handbook through the UKLA rules.

    See Chapter 3 Section 1.2 of your CISI Workbook

4. **C**   Relations with regulators is the FCA's Principle for Businesses No. 11.

    See Chapter 3 Section 1.2 of your CISI Workbook

5. **C**   The UK Corporate Governance Code recommends at least half of the board of FTSE 350 companies should be non-executive directors.

    See Chapter 3 Section 1.2.2 of your CISI Workbook

6. **D**   The UK Corporate Governance Code has developed through best practice rather than Acts of Parliament.

    See Chapter 3 Section 1.2 of your CISI Workbook

7. **D**   The business ethic of confidentiality means that you should not disclose information other than in the proper course of your business.

    See Chapter 3 Section 1.5.4 of your CISI Workbook

8. **A**   Half of the board of directors should be independent non-executive directors as part of a number of revisions to the UK Corporate Governance Code.

    See Chapter 1 Section 1.2 of your CISI Workbook

9. **C**   It is just CISI members who have to follow the rules of their trade association.

    See Chapter 3 Section 2.1 of your CISI Workbook

10. **C**   The UK Corporate Governance Code is concerned primarily with the stewardship role of directors.

    See Chapter 3 Section 1.2 of your CISI Workbook

11. **B**   The CISI Code of Conduct only applies to CISI members and is unlikely to be considered by the FCA.

    See Chapter 3 Section 2.1 of your CISI Workbook

Takeovers and Mergers

Questions

1. When a company attempts to take over another company, their aim is to acquire a legal control. Which one of the following percentages represents a legal control?

    A   More than or equal to 30%

    B   More than 50%

    C   More than or equal to 50%

    D   More than 75%

2. The latest day beyond which an unsuccessful offer cannot usually be extended after the posting of the offer document is:

    A   21 days

    B   28 days

    C   46 days

    D   60 days

3. The latest day an offer document can be posted after an offer has been announced is:

    A   1 day

    B   14 days

    C   21 days

    D   28 days

4. What is the maximum time between the announcement of a takeover and the target company's directors' initial response to shareholders?

    A   14 days

    B   42 days

    C   28 days

    D   21 days

5. The offeror launching a voluntary bid has acquired 9% of the shares of the target for cash in transactions occurring between six and nine months prior to the bid. What is the minimum price they must offer to remaining shareholders under the offer?

    A   The highest price the offeror paid in the last 12 months

    B   The highest price paid in the market in the last 12 months

    C   The highest price paid by the offeror in the last 3 months

    D   There is no minimum price required in the Listing Rules

6. **By when must a 1% share purchase be disclosed to the market in a takeover?**

   A   Immediately

   B   By noon the following business day

   C   By the end of the following business day

   D   Within two business days

7. **Control of a company is achieved in the context of the Takeover Code when a person (or persons) takes their stake in the company to more than:**

   A   20%

   B   25%

   C   30%

   D   50%

8. **Which of the following most accurately describes the normal contractual offer made to investors in a scheme of arrangement?**

   A   An offer is made to shareholders to buy shares

   B   A compulsory purchase of all shares is declared

   C   Shareholders are asked to vote on a proposed reconstruction

   D   Shareholders are given shares pro-rata to their current holding

9. **If a takeover offer is declared as unconditional, then which of the following is correct?**

   A   The offer is then closed to other shareholders

   B   The offer must remain open for a further 14 days

   C   The offeror must make immediate payment as promised

   D   The offeree may then decide to change their mind and hold out for a higher offer

10. **Which of the following best describes the application of the EU Takeover Directive?**

   A   EU registered target companies which are traded on an EU regulated market

   B   Any target companies which are traded on an EU regulated market

   C   Any target companies which are EU registered

   D   Any target company listed on an RIE or ROIE

11. **A company may appeal to which body against a decision made by the Competition and Markets Authority?**

   A   The Tax and Chancery Chamber of the Upper Tribunal

   B   The Competition Committee

   C   The Competition Appeal Tribunal

   D   The Regulatory Decisions Committee

12. **Which of the following fall within the scope of the Takeover Code?**

    I   A takeover

    II   A scheme of arrangement

    III An acquisition

    IV A statutory merger

A I only

B I and II

C I, III and IV

D I, II, III and IV

13. **Which of these parties would be most likely to be permitted to deal in shares of an offeree company?**

A Member of the offeree group of companies

B Shareholder of the offeree company

C Corporate broker of the offeree company

D Financial advisor of the offeree company

14. **Which of the following would be most likely to be exempt from the Takeover Code rule which prevents a person consolidating control in an offeree company?**

A A person holding 29% of shares purchasing a further 1%

B A person holding 31% of shares purchasing a further 1%

C A person holding 49% of shares purchasing a further 1%

D A person holding 51% of shares purchasing a further 1%

15. **If a company is required by the Takeover Panel to 'Put up or Shut up' then the company must do so by when?**

A 17:00 on the 28th day after a possible offer announcement

B 17:00 on the day after a possible offer announcement

C 17:00 on the 21st day after a possible offer announcement

D 17:00 on the 60th day after a possible offer announcement

16. **The Directorate General (DG) Competition investigates a merger and its Phase 1 investigation decides to proceed to a Phase 2 investigation. Which of the following is correct regarding the length of the Phase 2 investigation?**

A 25 days plus an optimal extension of up to 10 days

B 10 days plus an optimal extension of up to 25 days

C 125 days plus an optimal extension of up to 90 days

D 90 days plus an optimal extension of up to 125 days

17. **Which of the following best represents a possible defence available to directors of an offeree company against a hostile takeover offer?**

    A   A scheme of arrangement

    B   Finding a white knight

    C   A mandatory offer

    D   An open offer

18. **Under which of the following circumstances is it least likely that an offer announcement will be required under the Takeover Code?**

    A   Discussion of a possible offer has extended beyond a 'small number of parties'

    B   Reasonable grounds for concluding that an offer will be made exist leading to a 7% price increase in a day

    C   The holder of 15% decides to initiate a takeover bid

    D   The offeree company board is notified of a firm intention to make a takeover bid

19. **Dealings in relevant securities by the offeror made during an offer period must be disclosed by when?**

    A   12:00 on T + 1

    B   15:30 on T + 1

    C   12:00 on T + 2

    D   15:30 on T + 2

20. **Dealings in relevant securities by a shareholder with 3% holding in the offeree company made during an offer period must be disclosed by when?**

    A   12:00 on T + 1

    B   15:30 on T + 1

    C   12:00 on T + 2

    D   15:30 on T + 2

21. **The first closing day of a takeover bid is on which day?**

    A   Day 0

    B   Day 14

    C   Day 21

    D   Day 39

22. **An aggregate of at least what percentage interest in shares or more as defined by the Takeover Code represents control of a company?**

    A   15%

    B   30%

    C   50%

    D   75%

23. **Companies that are the recipients of decisions made by the Competition and Markets Authority:**

A   Cannot appeal

B   Can appeal to the TCCUT

C   Can appeal to the Competition Appeal Tribunal

D   Can appeal to the FCA

---

24. **Under the terms of the Takeover Code Rule 28 which is most correct regarding the inclusion of a profit forecast in an offer document?**

A   No profit forecast may be included in an offer document

B   Any profit forecast may only be for the following quarter

C   Any profit forecast must be reported on by the company directors

D   Any profit forecast must be reported on by the company's auditors and financial advisors

Answers

1. **B**   Legal control arises where a company owns more than 50% of another company. If a company owns 30% of the shares, this is known as effective control rather than legal control (> 50%).

      See Chapter 4 Section 2.8 of your CISI Workbook

2. **D**   The bid timetable will run for a maximum of 60 calendar days if an offer is unsuccessful. The timing may be extended if the bid is referred to the Competition and Markets Authority or if there is a rival bid.

      See Chapter 4 Section 2.16 of your CISI Workbook

3. **D**   Remember that all days in the Blue Book are calendar days.

      See Chapter 4 Section 2.16 of your CISI Workbook

4. **B**   28 days before documents posted, then 14 days for directors to respond, gives a total of 42 days after announcement.

      See Chapter 4 Section 2.16 of your CISI Workbook

5. **D**   As the bidder did not buy any shares in the last three months, nor buy 10% or more for cash in the last 12 months, there is no minimum price.

      See Chapter 4 Section 2.9 of your CISI Workbook

6. **B**   During the offer period, any purchases or sales of securities in the bidder or target company by a direct, or indirect, holder of 1% or more of those securities, must be disclosed to the market by no later than noon on the following business day.

      See Chapter 4 Section 2.10 of your CISI Workbook

7. **C**   Interest in voting rights of 30% or more gives effective control under the Takeover Code.

      See Chapter 4 Section 2.4.1 of your CISI Workbook

8. **C**   A scheme of arrangement asks that stakeholders vote on a proposed reconstruction of a company.

      See Chapter 4 Section 2.17 of your CISI Workbook

9. **B**   An offer must remain open for a further 14 days once it has been declared unconditional.

      See Chapter 4 Section 2.16 of your CISI Workbook

10. **A**   The EU Takeover Directive aims to harmonise EU takeover rules.

      See Chapter 4 Section 1.1.2 of your CISI Workbook

11. **C**   Appeals can be made to the Competition Appeal Tribunal about decisions made by the Competition and Markets Authority.

      See Chapter 4 Section 1.2.3 of your CISI Workbook

12.   **D**   The Takeover Code covers all changes of control however they take place.

See Chapter 4 Section 2.2.2 of your CISI Workbook

13.   **B**   Shareholders of an offeree company may buy or sell shares in the offeree company during an offer period.

See Chapter 4 Section 2.8 of your CISI Workbook

14.   **D**   Takeover Code Rule 5 restricts a person holding between 30% and 50% from consolidating their holding.

See Chapter 4 Section 2.8 of your CISI Workbook

15.   **A**   The Takeover Code Rule 2.6 requires that a firm announcement that they will make an offer or that they will not make an offer by 17:00 on the 28th day after the put up or shut up requirement.

See Chapter 4 Section 2.5.2 of your CISI Workbook

16.   **D**   Phase 1 of a DG competition investigation is 25 days with an extension of 10 days. Phase 2 would be 90 days plus up to 125 days extension.

See Chapter 4 Section 1.2.4 of your CISI Workbook

17.   **B**   White Knight defences would be a possibility for directors where they view a takeover as hostile. It involves finding an alternative bidder who may offer more agreeable terms.

See Chapter 4 Section 2.14.1 of your CISI Workbook

18.   **C**   In itself the decision to initiate a takeover bid would not require a formal announcement; if this has yet to become publicly known or suspected.

See Chapter 4 Section 2.5.2 of your CISI Workbook

19.   **A**   A disclosure by the offeror in a relevant security must be made without delay and at latest by noon on the day following the trade.

See Chapter 4 Section 2.10.1 of your CISI Workbook

20.   **B**   A disclosure by a shareholder with 1% or more holding in the offeree company in a relevant security must be made without delay and at latest by 15:30 on the day following the trade.

See Chapter 4 Section 2.10.1 of your CISI Workbook

21.   **C**   The first closing day is Day 21.

See Chapter 4 Section 2.16 of your CISI Workbook

22.   **B**   The Takeover Code defines 'control' as being an aggregate holding of 30% or more of voting rights.

See Chapter 4 Section 2.4.1 of your CISI Workbook

23.   **C**   Competition and Markets Authority appeals may be made to the Competition Appeal Tribunal.

See Chapter 4 Section 1.2.3 of your CISI Workbook

24.   **D**   Profit forecasts must be compiled by directors with due care and attention.

See Chapter 4 Section 2.15 of your CISI Workbook

Prospectuses

Questions

1. **Which EU directive contains the requirements for the documentation surrounding an IPO?**

   A Market in Financial Instruments Directive

   B UCITS Directive

   C Prospectus Directive

   D Public Offer of Securities Directive

2. **What is the maximum that a security's estimated market value can be before a prospectus is required for offers to the public?**

   A Less than £100,000

   B Less than €5m

   C Less than £700,000

   D Less than €12.5m

3. **The issue of which of the following securities is least likely to require the issuing of prospectus?**

   A Ordinary shares

   B Preference shares

   C Gilts

   D Corporate bonds

4. **Which of the following best describes the circumstances under which a company would be likely to require a prospectus for admission to the AIM market?**

   A Raising £5m from 150 or more non-qualified investors in any EU member state

   B Raising £5m from 150 or more qualified investors in any EU member state

   C Raising £0.5m from 150 or more non-qualified investors in any EU member state

   D Raising £50m from 150 or more qualified investors in any EU member state

5. **Which of the following is least likely to be considered to be a 'qualified investor' in terms of the need to produce a prospectus?**

   A An investment firm

   B The International Monetary Fund

   C A medium-sized business

   D A local authority

6. **Who has the primary responsibility for the contents of a prospectus?**

A   Auditor

B   Sponsor

C   Directors

D   Takeover Panel

7. **If, following the approval of a prospectus, there is a significant change in the company's state of affairs, which of the following would be most likely to be the case?**

A   The prospectus is no longer valid and a new prospectus must be published

B   The sponsor must disclose these changes via an RIS

C   The directors must disclose these changes via an RIS

D   A supplementary prospectus will be published

8. **When a class of shares not already admitted for trading is to trade for the first time, by when must the prospectus be made available to the public?**

A   At least 2 working days prior to the end of the offer

B   At least 6 working days prior to the end of the offer

C   At least 14 working days prior to the end of the offer

D   At least 21 working days prior to the end of the offer

9. **Where a prospectus has been issued electronically which best describes the publishing requirements of the issuer?**

A   A paper version must be made available free of charge on request

B   A paper version must be made available for a fee on request

C   A paper version must also be sent to all potential investors

D   The publishing requirements are fully satisfied

10. **The part of a prospectus which explains in non-technical language, the essential risks and features of the offering would best be described as:**

A   The appendix

B   The summary

C   The registration document

D   The securities note

11. **A sponsor is required to approve a prospectus for:**

A   Neither standard listings nor premium listings

B   Standard listings but not for premium listings

C   Premium listings but not for standard listings

D   Both standard listings and premium listings

Answers

1. **C**   The Prospectus Directive replaced the provisions of the Public Offer of Securities Regulations.

    See Chapter 5 Section 1.1 of your CISI Workbook

2. **B**   The limits of £200,000 and £700,000 are minimum market capitalisation for listing, and €12.5m is the balance sheet total for a non-MiFID professional client.

    See Chapter 5 Section 1.1.1 of your CISI Workbook

3. **C**   The issuing of gilts by the Debt Management Office will be exempt from the need for a prospectus.

    See Chapter 5 Section 1.1.2 of your CISI Workbook

4. **A**   Admission to the AIM market is only likely to require a full prospectus if it raises £5m from 150 or more non-qualified investors in any EU member state.

    See Chapter 5 Section 1.1 of your CISI Workbook

5. **C**   Small- and medium-sized businesses must self-certify if they are to be considered as qualified investors. The others would not be required to self-certify.

    See Chapter 5 Section 1.1.2 of your CISI Workbook

6. **C**   The directors are required to make a statement to the effect that they are responsible for all prospectus contents.

    See Chapter 5 Section 1.3.2 of your CISI Workbook

7. **D**   The supplementary prospectus must be submitted for approval as soon as practicable.

    See Chapter 5 Section 1.3.4 of your CISI Workbook

8. **B**   For reference, there a number of ways that a prospectus will be considered to be published.

    See Chapter 5 Section 1.3.5 of your CISI Workbook

9. **A**   A paper version must be made available free of charge if requested by the potential investor.

    See Chapter 5 Section 1.3.5 of your CISI Workbook

10. **B**   The three sections of a prospectus are the summary, the registration document and the securities note.

    See Chapter 5 Section 1.3.3 of your CISI Workbook

11. **C**   The term 'sponsor' applies to premium listings. Standard listings may require other advisers

    See Chapter 5 Section 1.3.3 of your CISI Workbook

Equity Capital Markets

Questions

1. **Which of the following is not a marketing operation?**

   A Rights issue

   B Introduction

   C Open offer

   D Offer for sale

2. **Which two of the following are rules that apply to a company applying for a listing through the UKLA?**

   I Minimum market capitalisation of shares must be £700,000

   II Minimum three years' trading history

   III At least 25% of shares available for trading publicly

   IV Pre-emption rights waived for a maximum of three years

   A I and IV

   B I and III

   C II and IV

   D II and III

3. **Alpha plc and Beta plc have identical operations. Alpha plc has a significantly lower free float. In identical trading conditions the shares of Alpha are, compared to Beta, most likely to experience**

   A An increase in volatility

   B A decrease in volatility

   C Identical performance

   D No similarities other than coincidental

4. **Which of the following types of listing does not involve the sale of shares?**

   A Placing

   B Intermediaries offer

   C Introduction

   D Offer for subscription

5. The management of Listable.com plc are planning an IPO for the company. They are seeking to realise some of their own personal investments, while at the same time raising new capital for future developments. Listable.com is an online supplier of specialist market information to paid-up subscribers. Management plans to sell 50% of their shares to raise around €15 million, and wants to raise a further €100 million in new capital. Which would be the most appropriate way of listing?

A   Placing and offer for sale

B   Placing

C   Introduction and offer for sale

D   Offer for sale and subscription

6. Which of the following best describes an offer for subscription?

A   The company issuing shares sells the shares directly to the investors

B   The company issuing shares sells the shares to an issuing house, which sells the shares to investors

C   The existing shareholders in the company sell shares directly to new investors

D   The existing shareholders in the company sell shares to an issuing house, which sells the shares to investors

7. When an individual acquires a material interest in a listed company, the company should be notified of this within

A   One business day

B   Two business days

C   Three business days

D   Four business days

8. What is the definition of a disclosable interest under the Disclosure Rules for a fund manager?

A   30%

B   15%

C   3%

D   5%

9. When an individual acquires a material interest in a listed company's shares, who must they notify within two business days?

A   The company

B   The market

C   The Takeover Panel

D   Department for Business Innovation and Skills

10. **How many market makers must there be for an issue of shares with a market value of £40m by a new applicant for listing?**

    A 0

    B 3

    C 2

    D 1

11. **For how long must a listed company keep its records in relation to its insider list?**

    A Three years

    B Five years

    C Six years

    D Indefinitely

12. **What is the main advantage for a company seeking to trade on the High Growth Segment of the Main Market, compared to a standard or premium listing?**

    A Lower minimum free float level of 10%

    B No requirement to produce a prospectus

    C A requirement for revenue growth of 20% (compound annual growth) over a three-year period

    D Exemption from EU regulated market requirements

13. **Which of the following is most closely linked to 'free float'?**

    A Market capitalisation

    B Share price

    C Shareholders' funds

    D Authorised share capital

14. **An insider list is required for which of the following?**

    I   Premium listing

    II   Standard listing

    III   AIM listing

    A I only

    B II only

    C I and II only

    D I, II, III and IV

15. **What is the minimum free float for a standard listing?**

    A No minimum

    B 10%

    C 25%

    D 50%

16. **What is the minimum market capitalisation on admission to a standard listing?**

A   No minimum

B   £700,000

C   £900,000

D   £1.5m

17. **A non 'quoted applicant' wishing to apply to AIM through an introduction will be most likely to need to produce which of the following?**

A   No documents

B   An admission document

C   A full prospectus

D   A supplementary prospectus

18. **Who is required to approve an AIM admission document?**

A   The FCA

B   AIM

C   The NOMAD

D   No one

19. **How many 'qualified executives' must a NOMAD employ?**

A   One

B   Two

C   Four

D   Ten

20. **If a company ceases to have a NOMAD, by when must it appoint a new one before it has its admission cancelled?**

A   Three days

B   One week

C   One month

D   Six days

21. **The High Growth Segment (HGS) is regulated by the:**

A   Financial Conduct Authority

B   Prudential Regulation Authority

C   Bank of England

D   London Stock Exchange

22. Premium listed companies are:

A   Not required to meet any UK or EU standards

B   Required to meet EU minimum standards only

C   Required to meet UK (EU equivalent) standards only

D   Required to meet UK super-equivalent standards

23. Standard listing is available to:

A   EU based commercial companies only

B   UK commercial companies only

C   UK or overseas commercial companies

D   Overseas commercial companies only

Answers

1. **B** Introductions do not result in finance being raised from the share issue and therefore are not marketing operations.

   See Chapter 6 Section 1.7.1 of your CISI Workbook

2. **B** Pre-emption rights may be waived by shareholders for a maximum of five years, minimum trading history only applies to premium listed companies. The minimum capitalisation for debt is £200,000.

   See Chapter 6 Section 2.8 of your CISI Workbook

3. **A** Free float relates to the amount of a company's share capital that is available for trading by members of the public. The lower the number of shares available to buy and sell, the higher the price volatility.

   See Chapter 6 Section 1.4 of your CISI Workbook

4. **C** An introduction only involves bringing existing shares onto a market. All the other answers will raise new finance for the issuer and are called marketing operations.

   See Chapter 6 Section 1.7.1 of your CISI Workbook

5. **B** A placing is the quickest and simplest way to raise new finance given the relatively small value of finance sought.

   See Chapter 6 Section 1.7.1 of your CISI Workbook

6. **A** This would be without the involvement of an issuing house, and is a method generally only used by investment banks or investment trusts who would have the experience in-house to administer all aspects of the issue.

   See Chapter 6 Section 1.7.1 of your CISI Workbook

7. **B** Once the investor reaches 3% and every time the investor changes the holding by going through a percentage point, eg 6.7% to 7.1%, the investor must inform the company by the end of the second business day following the day of trade, ie T + 2.

   See Chapter 6 Section 1.8.1 of your CISI Workbook

8. **D** The 5% level is for fund managers and other non-beneficial holdings. Disclosure is required at 5%, 10% and then every single percentage change above 10%.

   See Chapter 6 Section 1.8.1 of your CISI Workbook

9. **A** The investor tells the listed company. It is then the listed company that must tell the market via a Regulatory Information Service.

   See Chapter 6 Section 1.8 of your CISI Workbook

10. **A** The only requirement is that sufficient marketability can be assumed.

    See Chapter 6 Section 2.8 of your CISI Workbook

11. **B** Under the listing rules, the insider lists have to be kept up-to-date and recorded for the past five years.

See Chapter 6 Section 1.5.6 of your CISI Workbook

12. **A** Main advantage of HGS is reduced free float requirement. 20% CAG is a condition of access, but not necessarily an advantage.

See Chapter 6 Section 1.3.3 of your CISI Workbook

13. **A** It is common practice to only include the proportion of shares that are freely floating.

See Chapter 6 Section 1.4 of your CISI Workbook

14. **C** Insider lists are needed for both standard and premium listings under DTR rules.

See Chapter 6 Section 1.5.6 of your CISI Workbook

15. **C** The minimum free float needed for standard and premium listing is 25%.

See Chapter 6 Section 2.8 of your CISI Workbook

16. **B** The standard listing requires at least £700,000 equity listing.

See Chapter 6 Section 2.8 of your CISI Workbook

17. **B** An admission document is a reduced version of the prospectus.

See Chapter 6 Section 2.6 of your CISI Workbook

18. **C** The company's Nominated Advisor would need to approve the admission document.

See Chapter 6 Section 2.6 of your CISI Workbook

19. **C** There are a number of requirements that must be satisfied by a qualified executive.

See Chapter 6 Section 2.5.1 of your CISI Workbook

20. **C** A company's trading will be suspended if the company loses the services of its NOMAD.

See Chapter 6 Section 2.4 of your CISI Workbook

21. **D** The HGS is regulated by the LSE's HGS rulebook.

See Chapter 6 Section 1.3.3 of your CISI Workbook

22. **D** Premium listing requires an issuer to meet UK super-equivalent standards.

See Chapter 6 Section 1.1.3 of your CISI Workbook

23. **C** Standard listing requires issuers to comply with only EU-minimum standards.

See Chapter 6 Section 1.1.3 of your CISI Workbook

Practice Examinations

Contents

Unit 1 – Regulation

Practice Examination 1

(50 questions in 1 hour)

1. **What is the status of the FCA?**

   A   A crown agent

   B   An agent of the civil service

   C   A statutory regulator

   D   A company limited by shares

2. **Which of the following best describes s 21 of FSMA?**

   A   It is an offence for an authorised firm to issue a financial promotion

   B   It is an offence to issue a financial promotion unless it is issued by an authorised firm

   C   It is an offence to issue a financial promotion unless it is issued or approved by an authorised firm

   D   It is an offence to issue a financial promotion unless it is approved by the FCA

3. **When ensuring that communications made to retail clients comply with COBS rules, a firm must have regard to all of the following, except:**

   A   Past performance must be the most prominent feature

   B   Client's commitment

   C   Role of the information in the sale process

   D   Risks involved

4. **Which of the following is not one of the FCA's Principles for Businesses?**

   A   Market conduct

   B   Communications with clients

   C   Relations with government

   D   Financial prudence

5. **If an AIM company ceases to have a NOMAD, which of the following will occur?**

   A   The London Stock Exchange will automatically appoint a new one

   B   The company's shares will be suspended

   C   The nominated broker will fulfil the responsibilities of the NOMAD

   D   The company's AIM listing will be immediately cancelled

6. **When should a conflict of interest be disclosed?**

    A   When a specific conflict is not preventable

    B   When conflicts are identified and managed under a comprehensive conflicts of interest policy

    C   When engaged in business with a market professional

    D   When Chinese walls are in place

7. **A manufacturing company approaches an investment bank to manage an IPO of its stock. The investment bank arranges that a number of members of its own client base purchase blocks of the securities. This process would be best described as which of the following?**

    A   An offer for sale

    B   An offer for subscription

    C   A placing

    D   An introduction

8. **Which of the following does not represent an issue of shares for cash to the public when a company's securities first come to the marketplace?**

    A   Introduction

    B   Offer for sale

    C   Offer for subscription

    D   Rights issue

9. **Which of the following is the maximum penalty for conducting unauthorised regulated activities?**

    A   Two years' imprisonment or an unlimited fine

    B   Two years' imprisonment and an unlimited fine

    C   Seven years' imprisonment or an unlimited fine

    D   Seven years' imprisonment and an unlimited fine

10. **Which of the following is least correct true of a RIE?**

    A   Membership of the RIE does not confer authorisation as an investment business

    B   The RIE's business as an investment exchange requires it to have Part 4A permission

    C   The RIE provides an organised market framework within which transactions in investments can be effected

    D   The RIE will monitor the conduct of the market so as to prevent manipulation

11. **All of the following are DIEs, except:**

    A   Hong Kong Exchanges and Clearing Limited

    B   American Stock Exchange

    C   Tokyo Stock Exchange

    D   Euronext London

12. **Which of these communications would be least likely to have an exemption from the financial promotion rules under the terms of the Financial Promotion Order?**

    A   A prospectus for securities in a French company passported into the UK

    B   A prospectus approved by the FCA

    C   A promotion of units in an authorised unit trust

    D   A promotion made only to investment professionals

13. **Which of the following would be least likely to have committed a criminal offence under the terms of the Criminal Justice Act 1993?**

    A   A director who buys price-affected bonds in the company (which they are director of) while in possession of inside information

    B   A broker who discloses inside information to their doctor

    C   An employee of a company who sells price affected warrants while in possession of inside information

    D   A company which buys price-affected shares in another company while in possession of inside information

14. **When should a firm first notify its RIS about a share buyback?**

    A   Before the board meeting at which the decision is to be made

    B   Immediately after the board meeting at which a decision is made

    C   When executing the buyback

    D   Immediately after executing the buyback

15. **The Money Laundering Regulations for an employee of an authorised firm would be least likely to require which of the following?**

    A   That they must arrest the suspect

    B   That they must identify the source of any deposited funds

    C   That they must report suspicions of money laundering to their MLRO

    D   That they must check the identity of customers

16. **Which two of the following would be most likely to require a full prospectus?**

    I   A flotation of shares

    II   A rights issues

    III   A capitalisation issues

    IV   An employee share plan

    A   I and II

    B   I and III

    C   II and IV

    D   I and IV

17. **Who is the UK Stewardship Code primarily aimed at?**

   A   Directors

   B   Institutional investors

   C   Non-executive directors

   D   Custodians

18. **What is required before a public company (whose Articles of Association do not prohibit it from doing so) may reduce its share capital?**

   A   A special resolution in favour of the reduction only

   B   A special resolution in favour of the reduction which is then confirmed by the court

   C   A court order obtained by the company

   D   A public company may never reduce its share capital

19. **Which of the following is a per se professional client in relation to MiFID business?**

   A   A company with net assets of €30m, own funds of €3m and turnover of €20m

   B   A company with net assets of £5m

   C   A partnership with net assets of £4m

   D   A company with net assets of €5m, turnover of €20m and own funds of €2m

20. **For a retail client to be recategorised by an FCA firm as an elective professional client, all of the following requirements must be met, except:**

   A   The client must agree in writing to be treated as a professional client

   B   The firm can show that it has adequately assessed the client's expertise, experience and knowledge to waive protections provided for retail clients

   C   The firm has sent a clear written warning of the protections under the regulatory system which the client will lose

   D   The client must have performed at least ten significant transactions on the relevant market over the past year and have a portfolio exceeding €500,000

21. **Which organisation is least likely to take action to prevent a takeover?**

   A   Competition Appeals Tribunal

   B   Directorate General for Competition

   C   Competition and Markets Authority

   D   The Pensions Regulator

22. **Which of the following may cause an approved person to cease to be fit and proper?**

    I   Bankruptcy

    II   Breach of a conduct of business rule

    III Criminal conviction

    IV Disciplinary action by another regulator

    A I, II, III and IV

    B I, II and III

    C I, II and IV

    D I and III

23. **Under which circumstance would the Personal Account Dealing rules be most likely to apply?**

    A For a discretionary managed deal where no prior communication about the deal has been made to the relevant person

    B For a personal transaction in a life policy

    C For a personal transaction in the shares of a UK company which has been outsourced

    D For a transaction in a unit in a unit trust which is not managed by the relevant person or the person for whom the deal is undertaken

24. **Which two of the following transactions would give effective control of a company according to the regulations in the Takeover Code?**

    I   Acquisition of 11% of the shares when a holding of 6% was already owned

    II   Acquisition of 10% of the shares when a holding of 3% was already owned

    III Acquisition of 9% of the shares when a holding of 22% was already owned

    IV Acquisition of 32% of the shares when a holding of 1% was already owned

    A I and IV

    B I and II

    C III and IV

    D I and IV

25. **The latest day after the offer document is posted that an offeree company can make any announcements relevant to the offer is:**

    A 21 days

    B 39 days

    C 46 days

    D 60 days

26. **When an individual becomes aware that they have a major holding in a UK listed company, the company should be notified of this within how many business days after the individual becomes aware?**

   A   One business day

   B   Two business days

   C   Three business days

   D   Four business days

27. **In which of the following categories would a long-standing employee of an authorised firm who is an approved person with a wealth of €1m be likely to be categorised by a firm?**

   A   Elective retail client

   B   Per se professional client

   C   Elective eligible counterparty

   D   Elective professional client

28. **Which one of the following is not part of the regulatory system implemented by FSMA 2000?**

   A   FCA Principles for Businesses

   B   Financial Promotions Order

   C   Regulated Activities Order

   D   SEC rules

29. **What is NOT true of the offence of money laundering?**

   A   Maximum penalty for assistance is seven years and an unlimited fine

   B   It relates to the proceeds of any criminal activity

   C   Legislation covers institutional liability

   D   It is an offence to tip off a money launderer

30. **Which two of the following are true of the rules on personal account dealing?**

   I   It does not apply to life policies

   II   It forbids employees from dealing on own account in investments dealt in by the firm without permission

   III   It forbids employees from using another firm to effect own account transactions

   IV   It forbids employees from dealing in futures and options

   A   III and IV

   B   I and III

   C   I and IV

   D   I and II

31. **In relation to the rule on suitability, all of the following must be taken into account by the firm, except:**

    A   Knowledge and experience of the client

    B   The client's financial situation

    C   The client's understanding of the investment

    D   The client's investment objectives

32. **Who is responsible for ensuring the AIM rules are complied with on an ongoing basis?**

    A   The LSE

    B   The NOMAD

    C   The UKLA

    D   The FCA

33. **Which of the following would not be classed as insider dealing under the CJA?**

    A   Dealing in options in shares on the basis of inside information

    B   Dealing over-the-counter in shares on the basis of inside information

    C   Dealing in bonds on the basis of inside information

    D   Dealing in GDRs on the basis of inside information

34. **What is NOT a responsibility for a 'sponsor' under the Listing Rules?**

    A   Ensuring listing requirements are complied with

    B   Ensuring directors understand their responsibilities

    C   Ensuring that there is a market for the securities

    D   Getting the listing documents to the UKLA on time

35. **Which of the following is not a permitted cold call in an unwritten financial promotion?**

    A   The recipient has an established client relationship with the firm and envisages the call

    B   The recipient has an established client relationship with the firm

    C   The recipient does not have an existing relationship with the firm and the cold call concerns marketable packaged products

    D   The recipient does not have an existing relationship with the firm and the cold call relates to controlled activities in relation to readily realisable securities

36. **All of the following are excluded activities under FSMA 2000, except:**

    A   Dealing as a broker

    B   Employee share schemes

    C   Television programme

    D   Unremunerated personal representative

37. **Which of the following would be a disciplinary offence for an approved person?**

        I   A breach of FCA rules

        II   A failure to comply with a requirement of a personal account notice

        III   Provision of false information to the FCA

        IV   A failure to comply with an investigation by the FCA

A I, II, III and IV

B I, II and III

C I, III and IV

D II and III

38. **The FCA Code of Market Conduct contains which two of the following?**

        I   Legislation on market abuse

        II   Examples of conduct which does amount to market abuse

        III   Examples of conduct which does not amount to market abuse

        IV   Legislation on insider dealing

A I and III

B II and III

C II and IV

D I and IV

39. **All of the following are requirements for a firm to act in accordance with in order to satisfy the client best interest rule, except:**

A Honestly

B Fairly

C Clearly

D Professionally

40. **What is the maximum penalty for a director who permits financial assistance for the purchase of a company's own shares?**

A An unlimited fine

B An unlimited fine or two years' imprisonment

C An unlimited fine and two years' imprisonment

D An unlimited fine and seven years' imprisonment

41. **Which Statement for Approved Persons is being breached if you do not properly supervise staff or delegate tasks with appropriate supervision?**

A APER 1: Integrity

B APER 3: Proper market standards

C APER 4: Proper disclosure to regulators

D APER 5: Organisation of business for effective control

42. **Any of the following could request a BEIS investigation, except:**

    A   200 members or more

    B   Holders of at least 10% of the company's issued share capital

    C   Any shareholder who deposits £5,000 with BIS

    D   The company itself

43. **What is the correct order of the three stages of money laundering?**

    A   Positioning, layering, integration

    B   Placement, layering, integration

    C   Layering, integration, positioning

    D   Layering, placement, integration

44. **An individual has disclosed inside information to a friend but told them not to deal. The friend has dealt using the information received. Who is in breach of market abuse rules?**

    A   Neither

    B   Both

    C   Discloser only

    D   Friend only

45. **Which of the following best complies with the principles of corporate governance?**

    A   Directors' remuneration should have a performance related element

    B   Directors should be allotted share options

    C   Executive directors may set directors remuneration if it is subject to shareholder approval

    D   Details of executive remuneration should be contained in the Audit Report

46. **All of the following are set out as purposes of the Takeover Code in its Introduction, except:**

    A   The Code ensures that shareholders are treated fairly

    B   The Code ensures that the acquirer does not obtain an unfair commercial advantage over competitors

    C   The Code provides an orderly framework within which takeovers are conducted

    D   The Code is designed to promote the integrity of the financial markets

47. **Which one of the following is NOT a Principle of the Takeover Code?**

    A   All shareholders must be treated equally

    B   All employees must be consulted

    C   The target board must act in the interests of the company as a whole

    D   The takeover should not hinder the target longer than is reasonable

48. **Which one of the following price movements in offeree share price will give rise to the requirement for an announcement under the Takeover Code once a potential offeror is actively considering a bid?**

A   A 1% increase since the start of talks

B   An untoward movement in share price

C   A 5% increase since the start of talks

D   A 10% increase since the start of talks

---

49. **What is meant by the expression 'put up or shut up'?**

A   The Panel has the power to shut up a potential bidder unless it puts up a cash alternative

B   A potential bidder can be required by the Panel to declare whether or not it is intending to launch a bid

C   If the majority of remaining shareholders pass a whitewash resolution, a 30%+ shareholder will not have to make a mandatory bid

D   If a shareholder acquires a 30% shareholding, they must put up a cash bid for the remaining shares

---

50. **By when must transactions by 1%+ shareholders not connected to a bid during a takeover be declared?**

A   By 12:00 on the next business day after the transaction

B   By the end of the next business day after the transaction

C   By 15:30 on the next business day after the transaction

D   By the end of the second business day after the transaction

Answers

1. **C** The FCA is a statutory regulator. It is a company, but limited by guarantee, not by shares.

    See Chapter 1 Section 1.2 of your CISI Workbook

2. **C** A 'financial promotion' is described as 'an invitation or an inducement to engage in investment activity that is communicated in the course of business'.

    See Chapter 2 Section 3.1.1 of your CISI Workbook

3. **A** Past performance must not generally be given as the most prominent feature of any communication, as it is not a reliable indicator of future results.

    See Chapter 2 Section 3.2.2 of your CISI Workbook

4. **C** The relevant principle would have been relations with regulators.

    See Chapter 1 Section 2.2 of your CISI Workbook

5. **B** On the resignation of a NOMAD, the AIM company must seek to appoint a new one. The company's shares will be suspended for a short period awaiting the new appointment. Failing a re-appointment within one month, the listing will be cancelled.

    See Chapter 6 Section 2.4 of your CISI Workbook

6. **A** Under SYSC10, a firm should identify and manage conflicts of interest. Where conflicts are not preventable they are to be disclosed, but disclosure is not an alternative to trying to manage the conflict.

    See Chapter 2 Section 5.1 of your CISI Workbook

7. **C** A placing may be carried out as either a primary or a secondary offering. It generally represents the quickest and lowest cost option.

    See Chapter 6 Section 1.7.1 of your CISI Workbook

8. **A** An introduction is not a method of issuing shares for cash. It merely brings shares, already held by shareholders, into the marketplace. An offer for sale, an offer for subscription, (both known as marketing operation) and a rights issue all raise cash for the company.

    See Chapter 6 Section 1.7.1 of your CISI Workbook

9. **B** Section 19 of FSMA 2000, known as the general prohibition, states that the maximum penalty for carrying out regulated activities when not authorised to do so is two years' imprisonment and/or an unlimited fine, where found guilty in a Crown Court. As there is no answer with 'and/or' we assume you must choose 'and' since to get both jail and a fine would be the maximum penalty.

    See Chapter 1 Section 1.3 of your CISI Workbook

10. **B** The FCA 'recognises' and supervises RIEs and as such the business carried out as an investment exchange does not require further authorisation by the FCA.

    See Chapter 1 Section 1.2.6 of your CISI Workbook

11. **D** Euronext London Limited is an RIE.

   See Chapter 1 Section 1.2.6 of your CISI Workbook

12. **C** The Financial Promotions Order (FPO) allows certain exemptions from the financial promotion rules.

   See Chapter 2 Section 3.1.5 of your CISI Workbook

13. **D** The Criminal Justice Act (1993) offences apply to individuals only rather than to companies themselves. Individuals within the company however might by their actions fall under the Act.

   See Chapter 1 Section 5.2 of your CISI Workbook

14. **B** The general rule regarding disclosure of material new price-sensitive information – such as debt or equity issues and redemptions – is that it should be disclosed as soon as possible following any board decision. In this case, the firm should make an additional disclosure once it actually makes share purchases.

   See Chapter 6 Section 1.5.2 of your CISI Workbook

15. **A** Money laundering legislation does not require an individual to assist in the arrest of the money launderer.

   See Chapter 1 Section 4.4 of your CISI Workbook

16. **A** Employee share plans should not represent an issue to the public and, therefore, do not require a prospectus. A capitalisation issue represents a bonus issue of free shares to existing owners.

   See Chapter 5 Section 1.1.2 of your CISI Workbook

17. **B** The UK Stewardship Code has the objective of improving corporate governance by enhancing the dialogue between the shareholders (particularly institutional shareholders) and the board of the company.

   See Chapter 33 Section 1.3 of your CISI Workbook

18. **B** Although the Companies Act specifies three reasons why a reduction of capital may take place, these circumstances are not exhaustive. A private company requires shareholders to pass a special resolution only.

   See Chapter 1 Section 3.3 of your CISI Workbook

19. **A** For MiFID business a per se professional client must have two out of the following: €20m assets or more of net assets; €40m or more of net turnover; or €2m or more of own funds.

   See Chapter 2 Section 4.1.3 of your CISI Workbook

20. **D** The requirement of the quantitative test is ten significant transactions per quarter, over the past year.

   See Chapter 2 Section 4.2.2 of your CISI Workbook

21. **A** The Competition Appeals Tribunals will investigate appeals from companies against action from other bodies, such as the CMA, preventing a takeover

   See Chapter 4 Section 1.2.2 of your CISI Workbook

22. **A** An approved person must satisfy the FCA that they are fit and proper to carry out the controlled function. This would include the following considerations:

- Honesty, integrity and reputation
- Competency and capability
- Financial soundness

See Chapter 1 Section 2.7 of your CISI Workbook

23. **C** Where a deal has been outsourced, then the outsourcing firm must maintain records of any personal transaction.

See Chapter 2 Section 6.2 of your CISI Workbook

24. **C** Rule 9 of the Takeover Code deals with effective control and mandatory offers. Rule 9 states that where 30% or more of a company is purchased then effective control will be obtained.

See Chapter 4 Section 2.11.1 of your CISI Workbook

25. **B** Day 39 is known as the date of the last defence, when the directors of the target company (offeree) can defend the bid.

See Chapter 4 Section 2.16 of your CISI Workbook

26. **B** The vote holder notification (3% rule) states that the listed company must be notified within two business days of the individual becoming aware (T + 2).

See Chapter 6 Section 1.8.6 of your CISI Workbook

27. **D** They would need to have given their consent but would have met two of the three criteria of the quantitative test to be an elective professional client.

See Chapter 2 Section 4.2.2 of your CISI Workbook

28. **D** The Securities and Exchange Commission is the US regulator.

See Chapter 1 of your CISI Workbook

29. **A** The Proceeds of Crime Act applies to actions by individuals and provides that the maximum penalty for assisting a money launderer is 14 years and an unlimited fine. As a memory technique, it is easy to remember that for the offence of assisting a money launderer, we **double** the penalty of the other two main financial crimes (insider dealing and market manipulation) – and that there are 14 letters in 'money launderer'.

See Chapter 1 Section 4.2.1 of your CISI Workbook

30. **D** Personal account dealing rules aim to ensure that any personal transactions by a firm's employees do not conflict with duties owed to customers, and that after receiving the firm's permission, the employee notifies the firm promptly.

See Chapter 2 Section 6 of your CISI Workbook

31. **C** Although understanding of the investment is part of the knowledge and experience assessment, it is not an explicit criterion in its own right.

See Chapter 2 Section 7.2 of your CISI Workbook

32. **B** The Nominated Adviser is responsible for ensuring that the directors understand their obligations under the AIM rules, and that these rules are complied with.

    See Chapter 6 Section 2.5 of your CISI Workbook

33. **B** The insider dealing legislation only applies to deals on a regulated market or through a professional intermediary, therefore not over-the-counter.

    See Chapter 1 Section 5.1 of your CISI Workbook

34. **C** The sponsor's role is to advise the firm on listing requirements rather than to make a market on the securities.

    See Chapter 5 Section 1.3.2 of your CISI Workbook

35. **B** Existing clients must envisage receiving the call for it to be permitted.

    See Chapter 2 Section 3.2.4 of your CISI Workbook

36. **A** You must be dealing as principal and not holding yourself out to the market to be excluded.

    See Chapter 1 Section 1.6 of your CISI Workbook

37. **A** They are all examples of actions that would be considered disciplinary offences for an approved person.

    See Chapter 1 Section 2.3 of your CISI Workbook

38. **B** The Code of Market Conduct does not contain market abuse legislation. This is found in FSMA. It does not contain insider dealing legislation. This is found in CJA 1993.

    See Chapter 1 Section 7.6 of your CISI Workbook

39. **C** Financial promotions must be fair, clear and not misleading, but the clients' best interest rule is honestly, fairly and professionally.

    See Chapter 2 Section 2.1.1 of your CISI Workbook

40. **C** Two years jail **and** fined is the maximum sentence. The director may also be liable to the company for any losses suffered.

    See Chapter 1 Section 3.5 of your CISI Workbook

41. **D** The supervision of delegated tasks is actually covered in APER 6: Skill, care and diligence in managing the business whereas APER 5 is more concerned with the organisation of apportionment and delegation. However, APER 5 is the best available answer.

    See Chapter 1 Section 2.3 of your CISI Workbook

42. **C** One small shareholder (ie less than 10%) on their own could not ask for an investigation just by paying the fee.

    See Chapter 1 Section 3.4.1 of your CISI Workbook

43. **B** A money launderer will first need to place the illegal proceeds into the financial system; then layer it with proceeds from a clean source in order to separate the proceeds of crime from their original offence; and finally, integrate the proceeds back into the mainstream financial sector where they will appear legal.

    See Chapter 1 Section 4.1 of your CISI Workbook

44. **B** The individual has breached the rules on improper disclosure and the friend has breached the rules on insider dealing.

See Chapter 1 Section 5.2 of your CISI Workbook

45. **A** Directors should not be paid anyway, regardless of their performance, but should be incentivised to make the company perform well.

See Chapter 3 Section 1.2 of your CISI Workbook

46. **B** The Panel is not concerned with the commercial rationale aspects of a takeover.

See Chapter 4 Section 2.1 of your CISI Workbook

47. **B** Although it is a requirement of the Takeover Directive that employees be consulted, this is not contained in the six General Principles.

See Chapter 4 Section 2.3 of your CISI Workbook

48. **C** There is not a specified level, as for different shares and different market conditions the level representing an untoward movement may very significantly.

See Chapter 4 Section 2.5.2 of your CISI Workbook

49. **B** To ensure there is not a false market in the trading of a company's shares, the Panel may require a potential bidder to make a formal offer – 'put up'; or state that they do not intend to bid – 'shut up'.

See Chapter 4 Section 2.5.2 of your CISI Workbook

50. **C** The 1% shareholder disclosure rules are different for connected (12 noon) and unconnected parties (15:30) but both are on the business day following the trade.

See Chapter 4 Section 2.10.1 of your CISI Workbook

Practice Examination 2

(50 questions in 1 hour)

1. Which of the following is the minimum level of shareholding in a company which would necessitate the disclosure of dealings if the company was subject to an offer?

   A 1%

   B 3%

   C 5%

   D 10%

2. All of the following civil remedies are available to a client with whom a business has conducted unauthorised investment business, except the ability to:

   A Void the contract

   B Prosecute the business in question

   C Enforce the contract

   D Obtain damages for any loss suffered

3. What is the maximum penalty for insider dealing under CJA 1993?

   A Two years' imprisonment or a statutory fine

   B Two years' imprisonment and a statutory fine

   C Seven years' imprisonment or a statutory fine

   D Seven years' imprisonment and a statutory fine

4. Punishments available to the Takeover Panel for a breach of its rules include:

   A Censure

   B Suspension of listing

   C Suspension of FCA authorisation

   D Unlimited fines on the company directors

5. The UK Corporate Governance Code includes provisions relating to all of the following, except:

   A The determination of directors' remuneration

   B The independence of the Audit Committee

   C The control of inside information by a company

   D The role of non-executive directors in overseeing the decisions of the executive directors

6. **All of the following are not investments under the Financial Services and Markets Act 2000, except:**

    A   Gold

    B   Direct investments in property

    C   Options on sterling three-month interest rate futures

    D   Options on lead

7. **Which of the following is a way of obtaining authorisation to carry on investment business?**

    A   Being authorised by a DPB

    B   Being a member of Lloyd's

    C   Being authorised by the SFA

    D   Direct authorisation by the FCA

8. **All of the following are likely to appear on the agenda for a company's AGM, except:**

    A   Appointing directors

    B   Approving change in Articles of Association

    C   Approving the dividend

    D   Appointing the auditors and permitting the directors to set the auditors' remuneration

9. **Which of the following should you do if you have information concerning one client that would materially impact another client?**

    A   The firm should inform the second client that it holds this information

    B   The firm should cease to act for the second client

    C   The firm should disclose the information to the second client

    D   The firm should treat the information as confidential

10. **A mandatory offer will be required for a company in which two of the following circumstances?**

    I   An investor who previously owned no shares in the company acquires 30% of the company's shares from one shareholder

    II   An investor who previously owned 31% of the company's shares acquires any additional shares of the company from one shareholder

    III   An investor who previously owned 10% of the shares acquires an additional 8% from one shareholder

    IV   An investor who previously owned 10% of the shares acquires an additional 4% from one shareholder

    A   I and IV

    B   I and III

    C   I and II

    D   II and III

11. **All of the following are true of both RIEs and DIEs, except:**

    A They are both forms of investment exchange

    B Membership of neither is a means to obtaining authorisation as an investment business

    C They are both regulated by the FCA

    D They are both likely to provide a framework where prices traded on them can be assumed to be fair and open market prices

12. **What is the main purpose of a primary offering?**

    A Provide an official price

    B Enable companies to raise finance

    C Provide investors with the ability to trade

    D Enable companies to communicate with investors

13. **Which of the following most accurately describes the offence of insider dealing under CJA 1993?**

    A A civil offence

    B An offence against Stock Exchange rules

    C A criminal offence

    D An offence against best market practice

14. **The latest day on which an offer can be revised after the posting of the offer document is:**

    A 21 days

    B 28 days

    C 39 days

    D 46 days

15. **For a new applicant for listing planning to have debt and equity securities listed, what is the minimum total value of the securities to be listed?**

    A £900,000

    B £700,000

    C £500,000

    D £200,000

16. **All of the following are methods of a company raising new funds, except:**

    A Rights issue

    B Capitalisation issue

    C Placing

    D Offer for subscription

17. **Which one of the following is not an investment under the Market in Financial Instruments Directive?**

A   Contract for Difference

B   Commodity dealing

C   Spread betting in relation to sporting events

D   Underwriting money market instruments

18. **An s 793 investigation entitles a company to find out whether a person has had an interest in the company**

A   In the last three years

B   In the last two years

C   At anytime in the past

D   In the last year

19. **Which of the following is exempt from regulations covering financial promotions?**

A   Promotion to a company with net assets of £100,000

B   Promotion to investment professionals only

C   Promotion to a professional client in relation to MiFID business

D   Promotion to a retail client

20. **Which of the following best describes the requirements of a financial promotion?**

A   True and fair

B   Clear and not misleading

C   Fair, clear and not misleading

D   Reasonable

21. **Which of the following COBS rules is most likely to apply to a takeover or other related activity?**

A   Client assets

B   Lloyd's

C   Best execution

D   Chinese walls

22. **Which two of the following are true in relation to the rules on fair, clear and not misleading communications regarding investment services?**

    I   Only communications with retail clients need be fair, clear and not misleading

    II   Only written communications must be clear, fair and not misleading

    III Written communications with all clients must be presented fairly, clearly and must not be misleading

    IV Oral communications with retail clients must be fair, clear and not misleading

    A I and III

    B III and IV

    C II and IV

    D I and II

23. **Section 21 of FSMA requires a promotion in relation to securities to be issued or approved by an authorised firm. Which of the following is not exempt from this requirement under the Financial Promotions Order?**

    A A promotion to a high net worth individual

    B A promotion of a regulated collective investment scheme

    C A prospectus in accordance with the Listing Rules

    D A promotion to a sophisticated investor

24. **Which piece of legislation relates to the offence of money laundering?**

    A POCA

    B FSMA

    C CJA

    D JMLSG

25. **Which of the following is consistent with the principles of Corporate Governance?**

    A Directors should report on the company's progress to shareholders

    B Directors are ultimately accountable to the Chief Executive

    C Non-executive directors are made up of representatives of institutional shareholders

    D Executive directors set executive remuneration

26. **Which body is the UK competent authority with respect to regulated markets?**

    A PRA

    B FCA

    C HMRC

    D LSE

27. **To whom is the Tax and Chancery Chamber of the Upper Tribunal accountable?**

    A The Chairman of the Financial Conduct Authority

    B The Director General of Fair Trading

    C HM Treasury

    D The Ministry of Justice

28. **All of the following are true of Chinese walls, except:**

    A They can exist between employees of connected firms

    B They can exist between employees of the same firm

    C They must act as a barrier to the flow of information

    D They must be put in place by all FCA member firms

29. **When considering honesty, integrity and reputation as a part of the fit and proper test, which of the following is true? The FCA will:**

    A Only take into account if convicted in last ten years

    B Only take into account if convicted in last five years

    C Will not take into account spent convictions under any circumstances

    D May take into account spent convictions if relevant

30. **Employees of an authorised firm agree to act in conformity with all of the following, except:**

    A Their own regulatory obligations

    B The CISI Code of Conduct

    C The law on insider dealing

    D The anti-money laundering regulations

31. **All the following are requirements of COBS 12 on non-independent research, except:**

    A It must contain a clear and prominent statement that it does not follow the requirements of independent research

    B It must be clearly identified as such

    C It must contain a clear and prominent statement that it is not subject to prohibitions on dealing ahead of dissemination of research

    D It must contain a clear and prominent statement that the financial promotion rules apply as it is a form of marketing communication

32. **All of the following are criteria in the qualitative test for elective professional clients, except:**

    A Experience

    B Understanding

    C Expertise

    D Knowledge

33. **All of the following are required for a company to obtain a listing from the UK Listing Authority, except:**

    A Admission to the Official List

    B Admission to trading on an RIE

    C Two market makers

    D A free float of at least 25%

34. **Which of the following two offences are classified as market abuse?**

    I   Unlawful disclosure

    II   Misleading statements

    III Manipulating devices

    IV   Concealing devices

    A I and III

    B I and IV

    C II and III

    D II and IV

35. **All of the following are grounds for the FCA to use their investigatory powers, except which of the following?**

    A Where the FCA have good reason to do so

    B Where any person has committed market abuse

    C On a random basis of high risk firms

    D At the request of an overseas regulator

36. **Who will decide to take action against an authorised firm if it has breached the regulations?**

    A FCA enforcement division

    B HM Treasury

    C Panel on Takeovers and Mergers

    D Regulatory Decisions Committee

37. **Which of the following is exempt from s 19 of FSMA?**

    A Member of the London Stock Exchange

    B Trustee giving recommendations on investments

    C Local authority

    D Setting up an employees share ownership scheme

38. **When would a full PD prospectus be required?**

    A   Placing on NEX Growth Market to institutional investors only

    B   Main market capitalisation issue

    C   Offer for sale on main market

    D   3 for 1 bonus issue on AIM

39. **Which one of the following must always consent in writing to their client categorisation?**

    A   Retail client

    B   An elective professional client

    C   A per se professional client

    D   A per se eligible counterparty

40. **What is the maximum penalty for failure to report by an individual under the money laundering legislation?**

    A   14 years' imprisonment and an unlimited fine

    B   5 years' imprisonment and an unlimited fine

    C   2 years' imprisonment and an unlimited fine

    D   7 years' imprisonment and an unlimited fine

41. **A professional client may opt up to eligible counterparty if it has assets of at least:**

    A   €12.5m together with either €25m turnover or 250 or more employees

    B   There is no single requirement for elective eligible counterparties

    C   £10m irrespective of turnover, own funds or employees

    D   €20m together with €40m turnover or €2m own funds

42. **What is meant by the term 'equivalent third country business'?**

    A   A business that would be regulated by MiFID if the person was in the UK

    B   A business that would be regulated by MiFID if the person was in the EU

    C   A business that would be regulated by MiFID if the person was in Europe

    D   A business that would be regulated by MiFID if the person was in the EEA

43. **Which of the following cannot be prosecuted under insider dealing regulations as held with the Criminal Justice Act 1993?**

    A   An employee

    B   A shareholder

    C   A company

    D   A director

44. A CISI member is concerned that they are being required to act in a way that would breach the CISI Code of Conduct. They have already raised their concerns with their line manager, internal compliance, and audit committee but have not had their concerns resolved and feel that they have exhausted all internal option. What should they do next?

    A   Take their concerns to the police

    B   Resign their position

    C   Contact the CISI for advice

    D   Contact the FCA

45. Your firm has just advised a customer to invest in a specific company and the client has agreed to the investment. The proprietary traders at your bank also wish to purchase the same investment. Which of the following would be the correct procedure to follow?

    A   The orders must be executed fairly and in due turn

    B   The orders must be aggregated to give a fair price for all

    C   The firm must not perform its proprietary trade

    D   The client order must be executed before the firm's order

46. An investor is believed to have been unlawfully disclosing inside information and making false statements. Which piece of legislation is least likely to be relevant to any action against the investor?

    A   Criminal Justice Act 1993

    B   Market Abuse Regulations

    C   Proceeds of Crime Act 2002

    D   Financial Services Act 2022

47. Under which principle does the Panel have the power to force potential bidders out into the open?

    A   Principle 4: Prevention of false markets

    B   Principle 1: Equivalent treatment for all shareholders

    C   Principle 3: Offeree board must act in the interests of the company as a whole

    D   Principle 2: Sufficient time and information for an informed decision is provided

48. Under Rule 19 of the Takeover Code, who is ultimately responsible for the information in an Offer Document being prepared with the highest standards of care and accuracy?

    A   The sponsor

    B   The FCA authorised firm providing corporate finance advice

    C   The directors

    D   The shareholders

49.   By when must a bidder state the total number of acceptances?

A   Day 21

B   Day 46

C   Day 60

D   Day 100

50.   Which of the following is the maximum penalty for market abuse?

A   Two years' imprisonment and/or unlimited fine

B   Five years' imprisonment

C   Six months' imprisonment and/or maximum £5,000 fine

D   Unlimited fine

Answers

1. **A** During a takeover, the disclosure requirement applies to shareholders with 1% of the shares in either the bidding company, or the target company.

    See Chapter 4 Section 2.10.1 of your CISI Workbook

2. **B** Prosecution occurs in a criminal case and is not a civil remedy.

    See Chapter 1 Section 1.3 of your CISI Workbook

3. **D** The maximum penalty for insider dealing, where guilty in a Crown Court, is seven years imprisonment and an unlimited fine, known as a 'statutory fine'.

    See Chapter 1 Section 5.2 of your CISI Workbook

4. **A** The main punishment of the panel is censure as this damages the reputation of a firm.

    See Chapter 4 Section 1.1.1 of your CISI Workbook

5. **C** The Code is divided into five sections: leadership; effectiveness; accountability; remuneration; relations with shareholders.

    See Chapter 3 Section 1.1 of your CISI Workbook

6. **C** An option on the three-month sterling interest rate future (known as 'short sterling') is an option on a future which is a specified investment under FSMA 2000.

    See Chapter 1 Section 1.5 of your CISI Workbook

7. **D** The only way to become authorised (in the UK) is by direct authorisation from the FCA, although the 'passporting' route is also available for other EEA State authorised firms.

    See Chapter 1 Section 1.4 of your CISI Workbook

8. **B** Articles of Association are not frequently changed, and would require a special resolution.

    See Chapter 1 Section 3.6.3 of your CISI Workbook

9. **D** Keeping the information confidential would be the best way of managing a conflict of interest that has been identified by the firm.

    See Chapter 2 Section 5.2 of your CISI Workbook

10. **C** The mandatory offer is covered by Rule 9 of the Takeover Code which states that such an offer will be required if:

    - An investor acquires 30% or more of the shares of a company
    - An investor already owning 30% or more acquires further shares

    See Chapter 4 Section 2.11 of your CISI Workbook

11. **C** DIEs are not regulated by the FCA.

    See Chapter 1 Section 1.2.6 of your CISI Workbook

12. B The expression 'primary offering' describes when companies are coming to the market for the first time to raise finance.

See Chapter 6 Section 1.7.1 of your CISI Workbook

13. C Insider dealing, within Part V of the Criminal Justice Act 1993, is a criminal offence, carrying a maximum jail sentence of seven years.

See Chapter 1 Section 5.2 of your CISI Workbook

14. D The last revision day during a takeover process is Day 46.

See Chapter 4 Section 2.16 of your CISI Workbook

15. A Equity securities will have to have a market value of £700,000. Debt securities will have to have a market value of £200,000.

See Chapter 6 Section 1.4 of your CISI Workbook

16. B A capitalisation issue is the same as a bonus issue or a scrip issue where extra shares are given free of charge to existing shareholders pro rata to their current holding in order to reduce the unit price per share. It has the same effect as a stock split.

See Chapter 6 Section 1.7.2 of your CISI Workbook

17. C The Market in Financial Instruments Directive only covers spread betting in relation to financial assets (such as shares).

See Chapter 1 Section 8.2.5 of your CISI Workbook

18. A The s 793 notice covers a three-year period.

See Chapter 1 Section 3.7 of your CISI Workbook

19. B A financial promotion made only to investment professionals is given an exemption from financial promotion rules under the financial promotions order.

See Chapter 2 Section 3.1.5 of your CISI Workbook

20. C Financial promotions must be fair, clear and not misleading. This is in line with Principle for Businesses 7 Communication with Clients.

See Chapter 2 Section 3.1.3 of your CISI Workbook

21. D Effective Chinese walls would be required to stop information regarding the takeover spreading around the business. The other rules have no relevance to a takeover.

See Chapter 4 Section 2.4.1 of your CISI Workbook

22. B Oral and written communication with **all** customers must be 'fair, clear and not misleading'.

See Chapter 2 Section 3.1.3 of your CISI Workbook

23. B Any exemptions, under s 21 of FSMA 2000, with regard to financial promotions, do not have to comply with the detailed financial promotion rules. This, however, does **not** include the promotion of regulated collective investment schemes.

See Chapter 2 Section 3.1.1 of your CISI Workbook

24. **A** The Proceeds of Crime Act is the legislation that punishes those who assist, fail to report or tip-off a money launderer. The Joint Money Laundering Steering Group issue guidance notes on preventing money laundering.

   See Chapter 1 Section 4.1.1 of your CISI Workbook

25. **A** Directors are required to disclose in their accounts the application of the UK Corporate Governance Code and explain any breaches of the Code.

   See Chapter 3 Section 1.2 of your CISI Workbook

26. **C** UKLA does have the responsibility for approving and supervising sponsors, and its powers include the suspension and cancellation of admission to listing. However its primary responsibility is best reflected in answer C here, ensuring continuing obligations are met and enforcing them.

   See Chapter 6 Section 1.1 of your CISI Workbook

27. **D** The TCCUT is an appeals process for those subject to a Decision Notice from the Regulatory Decisions Committee (RDC). In order for it to be fully independent, it is separate from the FCA and HM Treasury and is part of the Ministry of Justice.

   See Chapter 1 Section 2.11 of your CISI Workbook

28. **D** The FCA does not directly require Chinese walls.

   See Chapter 2 Section 5.5 of your CISI Workbook

29. **D** Any spent convictions may be taken into account where relevant, but particular reference may be given to offences of dishonesty, fraud and financial crime.

   See Chapter 1 Section 2.7.1 of your CISI Workbook

30. **B** An employee of an authorised firm must follow all these areas, ensuring that they are fit and proper except for the CISI Code of Conduct which applies to CISI members only.

   See Chapter 3 Section 2.1 of your CISI Workbook

31. **D** Although the financial promotions rules will apply to non-independent research, there is no requirement to disclose this fact.

   See Chapter 2 Section 5.6.1 of your CISI Workbook

32. **B** The client's understanding is not explicitly stated in the qualitative test.

   See Chapter 2 Section 4.2.2 of your CISI Workbook

33. **C** The company must be admitted to the official list by UKLA, but also admitted to trading, by an RIE (such as the LSE). The minimum percentage of shares available to be brought and sold by the public (in free float) is 25% of the issued share capital; but there is no specified minimum number of market makers.

   See Chapter 6 Section 1.4 of your CISI Workbook

34. **A** The market abuse regime covers five abusive behaviours: Insider dealing, unlawful disclosure, manipulating transactions, manipulating devices, dissemination

   See Chapter 1 Section 7.1 of your CISI Workbook

35. **C** The FCA may launch an investigation on a number of grounds. These include:

   - Where the FCA have good reason to do so
   - At the request of an overseas regulator
   - Where a person has contravened specific provisions of the regulatory regime, such as market abuse

   See Chapter 1 Section 2.8 of your CISI Workbook

36. **D** Although the FCA will conduct the initial investigation, the decision to take action will usually be taken by the RDC.

   See Chapter 1 Section 2.10.2 of your CISI Workbook

37. **C** A local authority is an exempt institution.

   See Chapter 1 Section 1.7.3 of your CISI Workbook

38. **C** If admission to ISDX Growth Market (or AIM) is sought for only institutional investors then only an admission document is needed. Bonus issues/capitalisation issues don't require a prospectus.

   See Chapter 5 Section 1.1 of your CISI Workbook

39. **B** All the other classifications are automatic.

   See Chapter 2 Section 4.2.2 of your CISI Workbook

40. **B** The money laundering legislation, within the POCA 2002, states that failure to report money laundering carries a maximum penalty of five years' imprisonment and an unlimited fine.

   See Chapter 1 Section 4.2 of your CISI Workbook

41. **B** Size criteria only apply to per se professional client status.

   See Chapter 2 Section 4.2.3 of your CISI Workbook

42. **D** The territorial scope of all EU directives is to the European Economic Area.

   See Chapter 2 Section 1.2 of your CISI Workbook

43. **C** An insider is defined as an individual who has information in his possession that he knows is inside information, and knows is from an inside source. An individual would include a director, employee or shareholder of an issuer of securities, or a person having access to the information by virtue of their employment, office or profession. A person will also be an inside source if he receives the information directly, or indirectly, from one of the above and satisfies the general definition above.

   See Chapter 1 Section 5.1 of your CISI Workbook

44. **C** Members of the CISI are required to comply with the CISI Code of Conduct.

   See Chapter 3 Section 2.1 of your CISI Workbook

45. **A** We are not told in the question the exact timings of the deals and so we would be required to execute the orders fairly and in due turn as a means of controlling a conflict of interest.

   See Chapter 2 Section 5.5 of your CISI Workbook

46. **A** POCA 2002 relates to money laundering offences

See Chapter 1 Section 4.2 of your CISI Workbook

47. **A** Forcing a bidder out in to the open this should ensure that a false market does not emerge.

See Chapter 4 Section 2.3 of your CISI Workbook

48. **C** The directors always have ultimate responsibility, even if they delegate due diligence work to professional advisers.

See Chapter 4 Section 4.2.13 of your CISI Workbook

49. **C** Day 60 is known as 'the final day'.

See Chapter 4 Section 2.16 of your CISI Workbook

50. **D** As a civil offence, it is not possible to send a person to jail for committing market abuse.

See Chapter 1 Section 7.3 of your CISI Workbook

Practice Examination 3

(50 questions in 1 hour)

1. **Under Part 26, s 897 of Companies Act 2006, which of the following must be contained in the explanatory statement for a scheme of arrangement?**

    I   Details of the proposed arrangement

    II   The effect of the compromise or arrangement on the material interest of the directors of the company in so far as it is different to the interests of others

    III   The name and address of the company's solicitor

    IV   The name and address of the company's liquidator if in liquidation

    A   I, II, III and IV

    B   I and II

    C   I, II and IV

    D   I and III

2. **What is not one of the FCA's supervisory tools?**

    A   Monitoring

    B   Due diligence

    C   Diagnostic

    D   Preventative

3. **It is a requirement for the nominated adviser of an AIM company to:**

    A   Be on the approved advisers list

    B   Act as a NOMAD for one company only

    C   Own a minimum percentage of the company's shares

    D   Only act as an adviser for one group of investment professionals

4. **Which of the following is not an investment under the Regulated Activities Order 2001?**

    A   Foreign exchange contract

    B   Deposit at a clearing bank

    C   Certificate of deposit

    D   Spread bets

5. **Smith, a former director of ABC Ltd, rings up a market maker and provides him with false and misleading information as to the trading and prospects of the company, in order to facilitate a 'bear raid'. Which piece of legislation covers this offence?**

    A   Criminal Justice Act 1993

    B   Financial Services Act 2012

    C   Companies Act 2006

    D   Drug Trafficking Act 1984

6. **Which of the following is the best definition of material information in the context of material non-public information?**

    A   Disclosure of the information would be likely to have an impact on the price of the security or reasonable investors would want to know the information prior to making an investment decision

    B   Information which will cause the price of the security to move by in excess of 10%

    C   Information which is derived from confidential discussions between the receiver of the information and the issuer

    D   Information which is required to be released by an issuer

7. **Which of the following would not be regarded as an investment under the Market in Financial Instruments Directive?**

    A   Equity swaps

    B   Money market instruments

    C   Debentures

    D   Insurance contracts

8. **What is the deadline for a notification of a share purchase by a 1% shareholder during a takeover bid?**

    A   Close of play on the business day following the share purchase

    B   Close of play on the second business day following the share purchase

    C   12 noon on the business day following the share purchase

    D   12 noon on the second business day following the share purchase

9. **What is the maximum penalty in a Magistrates' Court for a breach of s 21 (restrictions on advertising)?**

    A   £5,000 fine

    B   Six months' imprisonment and/or a statutory fine

    C   £2,000 fine

    D   One year imprisonment and/or a statutory fine

10. **Responsibility for a financial promotion is taken by:**

A The appointed representative without exception

B The appointed representative and the authorised firm without exception

C The issuer and client appointed representative without exception

D The authorised firm without exception

11. **Personal Account dealing rules do not apply to which one of the following?**

A Administration staff

B Appointed representatives

C Approved persons

D Employees not involved in designated investment business who are not relevant persons

12. **For how long must the records of non-MiFID business for an FCA firm be kept?**

A Three years

B Five years

C Six years

D One year

13. **Which of the following is the best description of stabilisation?**

A A sidecar facility for fast markets to prevent excessive swings in price

B Excessive transactions on managed portfolios to earn commission income

C The inclusion of a cap and floor on floating rate debt

D A price support mechanism for the issuing house to allow clients to sell their securities back after an issue

14. **What percentage shareholding is deemed to give control according to the Panel of Takeovers and Mergers?**

A 29.9%

B 30%

C 40%

D 51%

15. **Which of the following cannot be classified as a per se eligible counterparty under the Client Categorisation Rules?**

A FCA authorised firm

B Own account commodity derivative dealer

C Pension fund

D An overseas individual who regularly deals off-exchange

16. **Which two of the following would be a breach of the Insider Dealing Legislation contained within the Criminal Justice Act 1993?**

    I   Selling on non-public price sensitive information

    II   A director dealing in the shares of his own company within two months of the announcement of results

    III A director of a company buying shares in an associated company

    IV   Purchasing of non-public price sensitive information

    A   I and II

    B   I and IV

    C   III and IV

    D   II and III

17. **Which two of the following are TRUE of a company's General Meeting (GM)?**

    I   A compulsory meeting called six months into the financial year

    II   It can be called by shareholders owning 5% or more of the shares

    III It can be called by shareholders owning 25% or more of the shares

    IV   It is any meeting other than an Annual General Meeting (AGM)

    A   I and II

    B   I and III

    C   II and IV

    D   III and IV

18. **Which one of the following is TRUE concerning the Board of Directors under the UK Corporate Governance Code?**

    A   The role of the Chairman and Chief Executive must not be performed by the same person

    B   The roles of Chief Executive and Finance Director must not be performed by the same person

    C   The roles of Chairman and a director of any other company must not be performed by the same person

    D   The roles of non-executive director and member of the remuneration committee should not be performed by the same person

19. **All of the following are true of the Money Laundering Legislation, except:**

    A   There are three recognised stages: placement, separation and integration

    B   Assistance, tipping-off or failure to report constitute offences under the legislation

    C   Firms must appoint persons to receive reports of any suspicious activity from employees

    D   Records must be kept for five years from the date to which they relate

20. **Which two of the following are Principles for Businesses of the Financial Conduct Authority?**

    I   Information for customers

    II   Independence

    III   Market Conduct

    IV   Skill, care and diligence

A I and IV

B I and III

C II and III

D III and IV

21. **Under s 59 of FSMA 2000, which of the following need not seek approval from the FCA?**

A Director

B Compliance officer

C Investment adviser

D Employee involved in general administration

22. **Which of the following is not considered to be designated investment business?**

A Funeral plan contract provider

B Advising on debentures

C Managing a portfolio of commodity derivatives

D Arranging a corporate finance deal

23. **When a firm writes to a retail client with regard to investment services all of the following are required with regard to the communication, except:**

A It is sufficient, clear, fair and not misleading

B It contains a fair and prominent indication of relevant risks

C It does not disguise, diminish or obscure important items

D It is sufficient to be likely to be understood by every member of the group to whom it is directed or by whom it is likely to be received

24. **Mrs Johnson and her immediate family have the following percentage shareholdings in XYZ plc, a listed company:**

    Mrs Johnson 1½%

    Mr Johnson (husband) ½%

    Additionally, Mrs Johnson holds options over ½% of XYZ plc's shares and over 1% of ABC plc a competitor company to XYZ plc.

    What notifications will Mrs Johnson have to make to XYZ plc concerning her total beneficial holding under the Disclosure and Transparency Rules?

    A   Disclosure 1½% actual direct holding

    B   Disclosure 2% family holding

    C   Disclose 2½% beneficial holding including options

    D   No disclosure to the listed company required

25. **A financial promotion coming from overseas is exempt from the FSMA rules if which of the following is the case?**

    A   It comes from outside the EEA

    B   It is not communicated to a person in the UK

    C   It is placed in the general media only

    D   It is communicated only via electronic media

26. **Which of the following is least likely to be considered to be an advantage to a company as a result of having its shares listed?**

    A   Access to public funds via the issue of shares

    B   The prestige given as a result of obtaining a quote which could assist trading prospects

    C   Increases the degree of management control over the company

    D   The ability to take over another company using only shares as consideration

27. **Which of the following is not true with regard to Chinese walls?**

    A   Chinese walls must be effective and prevent the flow of information

    B   Chinese walls may be established between a firm and its associates

    C   Chinese walls must be present in all regulated firms without exception

    D   Chinese walls may be established between divisions of the same firm

28. **All of the following could be valid reasons why permission for an introduction to the London Stock Exchange could be granted, except:**

    A   The shares are already listed on an overseas exchange

    B   The shares are the result of a merger between two listed companies

    C   To gain access to an offshore market to enable stock options to be granted

    D   The shares are widely held by UK investors

29. **Under the offence of insider dealing under the law as detailed in FSMA 2000, the role of the FCA is to:**

    A Undertake a criminal prosecution

    B Undertake a civil prosecution

    C Investigate the offence and pass the detail to the Crown Prosecution Service for prosecution

    D Set the level of the penalty fine

30. **Which of the following is a required function in the controlled functions?**

    A Apportionment and oversight

    B Internal audit

    C Finance director

    D Non-executive director

31. **An investigation notice issued under the Companies Act relates to an individual's holdings of shares over which time period?**

    A One year

    B Two years

    C Six months

    D Three years

32. **What is the percentage free float envisaged under the UKLA Listing Rules that would create a proper market?**

    A 25%

    B 10%

    C 20%

    D 30%

33. **The Regulatory Decision Committee has the power to do which one of the following?**

    A Refuse to extend a firm's permission to do regulated activities

    B Demand a copy of the firm's management accounts

    C Place a limit on a firm's foreign currency exposure

    D Require a firm to maintain a certain level of capital adequacy

34. **Which one of the following is true in relation to the application of COBS rules on personal account dealing?**

    A Approved persons only are covered

    B Only appointed representatives are covered

    C Only employees on the trading desk are covered

    D Employees and appointed representatives are covered

35. **The process where a deal manager ensures that in the immediate after market following the issue, the price remains above a minimum floor value, is known as:**

    A   Book building

    B   Stabilisation

    C   Headroom

    D   Novation

36. **XYZ Media Ltd has approached you to sell its entire share capital, to whom may you issue a Memorandum of Information?**

    A   Anybody

    B   Qualified investors only

    C   Professional investor only

    D   Professional investors and high net worth individuals

37. **Information which a firm has received in writing can be relied upon under FCA rules if:**

    I   The person who provided the information is unconnected to the firm

    II   The person who provided the information is associated with the firm

    III   The person who provided the information is a professional firm

    IV   The person who provided the information is an expert

    A   I and III

    B   II and IV

    C   III and IV

    D   I and IV

38. **If a firm receives material information about one client that would materially impact a second client, the firm should:**

    A   Inform the second client

    B   Cease to act for one of the clients

    C   Review the firm's Chinese walls

    D   Treat the information as confidential

39. **A listed firm offering shares via a placing would best be described as:**

    A   Issuing shares to certain investors only

    B   Offering new shares for cash to all existing shareholders

    C   Offering free new shares to all shareholders

    D   Offering shares to all shareholders

40. **Which two of the following would be classified as investment businesses under the Financial Services and Markets Act 2000?**

    I   A company dealing as principal only for themselves

    II   A daily newspaper giving investment advice

    III A unit trust only investing in property

    IV A trustee giving investment advice

A I and IV

B II and III

C II and IV

D III and IV

41. **The insider dealing legislation under CJA 93 relates to:**

A Unquoted shares

B Fixed odds bets

C FX forward contracts

D Contracts for Difference

42. **Individuals accused of breaching s 19 and conducting an activity without authorisation would best be able to defend themselves by claiming:**

A They were investing on their own behalf

B They were being supervised by an authorised person

C They have applied for authorisation and are awaiting sign off from the FCA

D They did not expect to make a profit from their dealing

43. **Which one of the following is a Principle of the Takeover Code?**

A All parties to a bid must act with skill, care and diligence

B The offeror must not be hindered in the conduct of its affairs for longer than is reasonable

C The board of the target must act in the interests of the company as a whole

D The bidder must act with financial prudence

44. **What is the waiting period for a potential bidder who has confirmed that they are currently not making an offer to launch a subsequent bid?**

A One month

B Three months

C Six months

D One year

45.   All of the following must be included in the announcement of a takeover bid, except:

A   Terms of the bid including any conditions applied to the bid

B   Identity of the offeror

C   Holdings of the target in the offeror company

D   Confirmation that a cash offer can be fulfilled

46.   All of the following are acceptable conditions that a bidder may impose on their bid, except:

A   That at least 90% of the remaining shareholders say yes to the bid

B   That the Competition and Markets Authority clears the bid

C   That the bidder's shareholders approve the issue of new securities to finance the bid

D   That following consultation, a majority of the target's employees approve the bid

47.   Which of the following correctly describes the status of full list and AIM companies?

A   Full list companies trade on an exchange regulated market whereas AIM companies trade on an EU regulated market

B   Full list companies trade on an EU regulated market whereas AIM companies trade on an exchange regulated market

C   Both full list and AIM companies trade on an exchange regulated market

D   Both full list and AIM companies trade on an EU regulated market

48.   Which is the body to whom you may appeal a Decision Notice?

A   Upper Tribunal (Tax and Chancery Chamber)

B   RDC

C   FOS

D   FSCS

49.   Which TWO of the following are situations set out in the Listing Rules that permit a company delay the announcement of price sensitive information?

I   So as not to prejudice its legitimate interest if the delay is unlikely to mislead the public

II   If the Panel on Takeovers and Mergers gives permission not to make an announcement

III   If the matters concerned are subject to negotiation and confidentiality can be maintained

IV   If disclosure is made to registered intermediaries only

A   I and III

B   I and II

C   II and IV

D   III and IV

50. **Under which circumstances would a company listing on AIM not require a full prospectus?**

        I   An offer for subscription

        II   A placing

        III   An offer for sale

        IV   An introduction

A I and III

B II and IV

C I, II and III

D I, II, III and IV

Answers

1. **B**   Section 897 requires the company to give all information reasonably necessary to enable shareholders and creditors to vote. The name and address of the solicitor or liquidator would be irrelevant.

    See Chapter 1 Section 3.1.1 of your CISI Workbook

2. **B**   The FCA set out four groups of supervisory tools in the Handbook. The other one not shown is remedial.

    See Chapter 1 Section 2.4.1 of your CISI Workbook

3. **A**   The London Stock Exchange maintains a list of the advisers who are approved to be NOMADS.

    See Chapter 6 Section 2.4 of your CISI Workbook

4. **A**   Foreign exchange contracts are only covered by the Regulated Activities Order if they are speculative forward contracts or options on Forex.

    See Chapter 1 Section 1.4 of your CISI Workbook

5. **B**   Financial Services Act 2012 covers offences of misleading information.

    See Chapter 1 Section 7.1 of your CISI Workbook

6. **A**   To be material, it would need to affect the decisions of users. It would be a breach of the Disclosure Rules and CISI Code of Conduct to disclose or inappropriately use material non-public information.

    See Chapter 1 Section 5.1 of your CISI Workbook

7. **D**   Insurance is covered under its own EU Directive.

    See Chapter 1 Section 8.2.5 of your CISI Workbook

8. **C**   This is known as accelerated disclosure, and is due to the takeover bid. The Disclosure Rules require disclosure to a listed company by a shareholder acquiring a 3% holding (or increasing it through a whole percentage point) by the end of the second business day after the trade; during the takeover bid any acquisition of shares by a 1% holder must be notified to the market by 12 noon on the next business day. Although the question does not tell us whether the 1% shareholder is a connected party, the 15:30 deadline for unconnected parties is not available.

    See Chapter 4 Section 2.10.1 of your CISI Workbook

9. **B**   Section 21 of FSMA 2000 states that any advertisement in the UK must be issued, or approved, by an authorised firm. Contravention will lead to a penalty of six months' imprisonment and/or a fine of £5,000 (the statutory fine) if found guilty in a Magistrates' Court.

    See Chapter 2 Section 3.1.2 of your CISI Workbook

10. **D** A difficult question to interpret what the examiner believes is the correct answer. The COBS rules state that it applies to firms when the financial promotion is carried out by themselves or their appointed representatives in the UK. We believe that the firm alone having ultimate responsibility is probably the best available answer as appointed representatives are exempt persons not directly regulated by the FCA.

See Chapter 2 Section 3.1.1 of your CISI Workbook

11. **D** The Conduct of Business Sourcebook personal account dealing rules only apply to employees doing designated investment business.

See Chapter 2 Section 6.1 of your CISI Workbook

12. **A** The general record keeping requirement of the FCA states three years for non-MiFID business and five years for MiFID business. The money laundering regulations state that 'cash' records must be maintained for at least five years.

See Chapter 1 Section 2.5.11 of your CISI Workbook

13. **D** Stabilisation is where the firm will support trading in the security immediately after its issue, ie a price support mechanism.

See Chapter 1 Section 7.7.3 of your CISI Workbook

14. **B** The level of ownership that is deemed 'effective control' is ownership of at least 30% (ie $\geq 30\%$). At this level, a mandatory offer/bid is required.

See Chapter 4 Section 2.8 of your CISI Workbook

15. **D** The overseas individual would need to the authorised or regulated under the law of the EU or an EEA state.

See Chapter 2 Section 4.1.3 of your CISI Workbook

16. **B** Item II would only be a breach of the Listing Rules' Model Code on Director's Share Dealings but we do not know if the director did have inside information. Item III would only be an offence if they were acting on inside information.

See Chapter 1 Section 5.1 of your CISI Workbook

17. **C** Annual General Meetings (AGMs) need to be held once every calendar year (with a maximum gap between meetings of 15 months). General Meetings (GMs) are in addition to AGMs – they can be called by shareholders owning 5% or more of the shares, or by director, to discuss matters in addition to the AGM.

See Chapter 1 Section 3.6 of your CISI Workbook

18. **A** The roles of Chairman and Chief Executive should be kept separate.

See Chapter 3 Section 1.2.1 of your CISI Workbook

19. **A** The three stages are placement, **layering** and integration.

See Chapter 1 Section 4.1 of your CISI Workbook

20. **D** Market Conduct is the fifth Principle for Businesses and Skill, Care and Diligence is the second Principle for Businesses.

See Chapter 1 Section 2.2 of your CISI Workbook

21. **D** Approved person status is required for employees involved in controlled functions within an authorised firm. General administration responsibilities are not classified as a controlled function.

See Chapter 1 Section 2.6.1 of your CISI Workbook

22. **A** Funeral plans are retail savings products to pay for funeral expenses. Although they are on the list of 'specified' investments under the Regulated Activities Order, they are not considered part of designated investments.

See Chapter 1 Section 1.4 of your CISI Workbook

23. **D** The requirement states the communication should be likely to be understood by the **average** member of the group.

See Chapter 2 Section 3.2.1 of your CISI Workbook

24. **D** The following must be taken into account when considering necessary disclosures for the register of material interests:

- The stakeholder's **own position**
- Any shares controlled by the stakeholder e.g. through their **spouse**

Options or other derivatives on shares. (However options on unconnected companies such as ABC plc are irrelevant.)

As the total beneficial holding is less than 3%, no disclosure is required.

See Chapter 6 Section 1.8.1 of your CISI Workbook

25. **B** An example of a promotion which is not communicated to a person in the UK would be a foreign newspaper available at UK airports for foreign visitors.

See Chapter 2 Section 3.1.1 of your CISI Workbook

26. **C** A listing is a way that a company can raise funds via the issue of shares. Gaining a listing may assist trading prospects by increasing the liquidity of the share, especially if the share is listed on the Full List. Being able to take over a company using only shares as consideration, rather than cash, means that a company can expand without needing to raise finance. By offering shares to external investors control over the company by management is unlikely to be increased.

See Chapter 6 Section 1.1.3 of your CISI Workbook

27. **C** Chinese walls are not mandatory but when used they must be effective.

See Chapter 2 Section 5.5 of your CISI Workbook

28. **C** An introduction to the LSE involves introducing shares for trading to the market of the London Stock Exchange for the first time. It does not involve raising cash for the issuing company, since the shares are already held by shareholders. Granting stock options is not a valid reason why the LSE might give permission for this to occur.

See Chapter 6 Section 1.7.1 of your CISI Workbook

29. **B** FSMA 2000 contains the civil offence of market abuse and empowers the FCA to bring civil proceedings against offenders.

See Chapter 1 Section 7.1 of your CISI Workbook

30. **A**   Apportionment and oversight is the other required controlled function along with the Compliance Officer and MLRO.

See Chapter 1 Section 2.6.1 of your CISI Workbook

31. **D**   An s 793 Investigation Notice allows the company to ask an individual whether or not they held shares in the company in the last three years.

See Chapter 1 Section 3.7 of your CISI Workbook

32. **A**   25% is the amount set out in the UKLA guidelines.

See Chapter 6 Section 1.4 of your CISI Workbook

33. **A**   The other powers are direct regulatory powers of the FCA or the PRA.

See Chapter 1 Section 2.10.2 of your CISI Workbook

34. **D**   The rules potentially apply to all employees and also to the appointed representatives of the firm as these are the firm's responsibility under COBS.

See Chapter 2 Section 6.1 of your CISI Workbook

35. **B**   Price stabilisation is where the fund manager supports trading in the security immediately after the issue.

See Chapter 1 Section 5.3.2 of your CISI Workbook

36. **D**   This is a difficult question to interpret from the limited information provided, it is relating to the financial promotion order exemptions of investment professionals and high net worth individuals. A private limited company would be an unlisted security.

See Chapter 2 Section 3.1.5 of your CISI Workbook

37. **A**   The requirement is to be **unconnected** and **competent**.

See Chapter 2 Section 2.3 of your CISI Workbook

38. **D**   Principle 8 and SYSC IO require the firm to mange the conflict and operate effective arrangements to prevent a material risk of damage to client's interest.

See Chapter 2 Section 5.1 of your CISI Workbook

39. **A**   A placing is an offer of shares to a limited number of potential shareholders such as institutional investors.

See Chapter 6 Section 1.7.1 of your CISI Workbook

40. **D**   Trustees are only exempt if they do not give investment advice or are not separately remunerated.

See Chapter 1 Section 1.7 of your CISI Workbook

41. **D**   The CJA'93 relates to securities traded on a regulated market or through a professional intermediary. It therefore does not relate to unquoted shares, betting companies or the FX market.

See Chapter 1 Section 5.1 of your CISI Workbook

42.   **A**   This would be the defence of dealing as principal (ie for their own account) and not holding themselves out to the market.

See Chapter 1 Section 1.6 of your CISI Workbook

43.   **C**   The target board are not allowed to do any frustrating actions of the bid without shareholder consent. Note that it is the offeree who must not be hindered longer than is reasonable.

See Chapter 4 Section 2.3 of your CISI Workbook

44.   **C**   Note that this was only a 'potential bidder' and therefore when given a 'put up or shut up' ultimatum by the Panel, if they have declined to make a proper bid they have to wait six months. It is a failed bidder who has to wait 12 months to relaunch a bid.

See Chapter 4 Section 2.5.2 of your CISI Workbook

45.   **C**   It is holdings in the target company by the offeror that must be disclosed (ie how much has the bidder already bought of the target company).

See Chapter 4 Section 2.5.2 of your CISI Workbook

46.   **D**   Although the Takeover Directive introduced the need to consult employees, they do not have a say in the success of the takeover.

See Chapter 4 Section 2.5.2 of your CISI Workbook

47.   **B**   The AIM market is deliberately classified as an exchange regulated market so that its admission requirements are lower and more suited to start-up companies.

See Chapter 6 Section 1.2.1 of your CISI Workbook

48.   **A**   Within 28 calendar days of receiving a Decision Notice, the recipient can appeal it to the TCCUT.

See Chapter 1 Section 2.11 of your CISI Workbook

49.   **A**   The UKLA will determine whether disclosure needs to be made not the Panel. The UKLA are concerned that everyone should know a key piece of information, not just intermediaries.

See Chapter 6 Section 1.5.3 of your CISI Workbook

50.   **B**   Introductions and placings on AIM will not require a full prospectus but may produce an abbreviated form as prescribed by AIM rules.

See Chapter 6 Section 2.6 of your CISI Workbook

Practice Examination 4

(50 questions in 1 hour)

1. **All of the following activities would represent money laundering, except:**

    A   Using the proceeds of a robbery to buy a car and then selling the car shortly afterwards

    B   Separating a sum of money, obtained through drug dealing, into several different currencies payable into several different accounts

    C   Using money from a protection racket to buy a cash-based business. The business then deliberately overpays its tax liability for the year

    D   Making a profit from a drug deal

2. **Which one of the following is not a specified investment?**

    A   An option over gold

    B   An ordinary share

    C   A premium bond

    D   An interest rate swap

3. **Which of the following statements is least correct in relation to a firm's money laundering reporting officer (MLRO)?**

    A   The MLRO's responsibilities are set out in SYSC

    B   The MLRO must be an approved person

    C   The MLRO must be sufficiently independent to act on his own authority

    D   The MLRO and the nominated officer must be separate persons

4. **In order to attain approval, an individual must usually satisfy which two of the following?**

    I   Pass the relevant examination

    II   Pass a minimum of five GCSEs

    III   Meet the requirements of an internal assessment

    IV   Become a member of the Chartered Institute for Securities and Investment

    A   I and III

    B   II and III

    C   II and IV

    D   III and IV

5. **Which of the following is least correct regarding the Tax and Chancery Upper Tribunal?**

   A   A person who receives a Decision Notice can refer the matter to the Tribunal within 28 days

   B   A third party who receives a copy of a Decision Notice can refer it to the Tribunal within 28 days

   C   The Financial Services and Markets Tribunal is part of the FCA, although constructed using Chinese walls

   D   The Tribunal may utilise new evidence not available at earlier hearings

6. **Which of the following is not one of the Principles for Businesses?**

   A   Management and Control

   B   Customer: Relationship of Trust

   C   Market Prudence

   D   Relations with Regulators

7. **Section 793 of the Companies Act 2006 is applicable to:**

   A   Public companies

   B   Listed companies

   C   Private companies

   D   All of the above

8. **A company issuing only wholesale securities may be exempt from the need to produce a prospectus. The minimum denomination of such a security is:**

   A   €1,000

   B   €10,000

   C   €100,000

   D   €1,000,000,000

9. **Which of the following is not a direct power of the FCA?**

   A   Public censure

   B   Seek an injunction

   C   Unlimited fine

   D   Winding up of a company that has breached a rule

10. **When should a conflict of interest be disclosed?**

   A   When the conflict is not preventable

   B   When acting for a third party

   C   To a market professional

   D   When Chinese walls are in place

11. **An offeror in a mandatory bid situation has made the following recent purchases in the target company's shares. If the market price of the shares was 80p per share when the offeror was required to launch the mandatory bid, what price can the offeror bid for the shares?**

WHEN PURCHASED	PRICE PAID
11 months ago	85p per share
Five months ago	82p per share
Two months ago	84p per share

A 84p per share

B 82p per share

C 85p per share

D 80p per share

12. **Which of the following would not ordinarily be classified as a per se eligible counterparty?**

A Large businesses

B FCA firm

C Central bank

D Supranational organisation

13. **Which statement best describes the role of a non-executive director?**

A A person responsible for the day-to-day management of the company

B A person acting as a director for the company who is not entitled to a salary

C A person responsible for providing an overview of the company's activities and supervising other directors

D A person responsible for deciding the salaries of all senior management personnel

14. **Which of the following may be exempt from the Personal Account Dealing rules?**

A Eligible counterparty

B Market maker

C Institutional shareholder

D Life policy personal transactions

15. **Which of the following would be classified as a designated investment?**

A Funeral plan contract

B Unit in a Collective Investment Scheme

C Bank deposit

D Residential mortgage

16. What is the role of the role of the NOMAD?

A   Marketing the new shares of a listed company

B   Underwriting services for an AIM company

C   Regulatory advisory services to an AIM company

D   Arranging a book building exercise for an IPO

17. Which of the following methods would not be acceptable under the EU Directive on money laundering with regard to verifying a client's identity?

A   Checking the electoral role

B   Relying on others to vouch for the identification

C   Visiting the client's home

D   Checking a current bank statement

18. When does the COBS rule on suitability apply?

A   When a firm makes a basic scripted advice for stakeholder products

B   For all retail clients

C   When a firm makes a personal recommendation in relation to a designated investment

D   When a retail client performs an execution only trade in derivatives

19. When a firm issues a financial promotion, it must do all of the following, except:

A   Be checked by an individual with appropriate expertise

B   Ensure that the advertisement is fair, clear and not misleading

C   Ensure that the advertisement identifies it as being approved by the FCA

D   Ensure that the advertisement identifies the firm as the issuer

20. What is the maximum penalty for a breach of the Bribery Act by a commercial organisation?

A   Ten years' imprisonment and an unlimited fine

B   Seven years' imprisonment and an unlimited fine

C   An unlimited fine

D   Five years' imprisonment and an unlimited fine

21. Which of the following is most correct in relation to the FCA Financial Promotion Rules?

A   The rules do not apply to non-investment insurance contracts

B   All financial promotions must be issued by an authorised firm

C   Financial promotions must not be made for derivatives

D   An email is a non-written financial promotion

22. **Which of the following is most likely to prosecute for insider dealing?**

    A   BIS

    B   HMT

    C   FCA

    D   LSE

23. **If a firm has a conflict that it is unable to prevent, it must:**

    A   Disclose it in sufficient detail for the client to take an informed decision

    B   Establish Chinese walls

    C   Cease to be a market maker in the security, subject to the conflict of interest

    D   Operate a policy of independence

24. **Which of the following is the penalty for market abuse?**

    A   Suspension of listing

    B   Liquidation of the firm

    C   An unlimited fine

    D   Seven years' imprisonment

25. **Which of the following would not normally be classified as a retail client for non-MiFID business?**

    A   Approved person

    B   Company with net assets of more than £2m

    C   Trust with assets of less than £5m

    D   Company with share capital of more than £5m

26. **Which of the following best describes the purpose of SYSC?**

    A   Ensure directors are approved

    B   Ensure directors know their responsibilities with regard to controlling the company

    C   To dictate how a firm must delegate its responsibilities

    D   To govern the appointment of directors

27. **Which of the following statements concerning Chinese walls is false?**

    A   May be operated by firms with more than one division

    B   Are a way of monitoring conflicts of interest

    C   Are internal arrangements which restrict the flow of confidential information

    D   COBS rules specify use of Chinese walls for investment management firms

28. **All the following are documents required under the Prospectus Directive rules, except:**

    A Annual report and accounts

    B Registration document

    C Summary document

    D Securities note

29. **If a significant change of affairs has taken place after a prospectus has already been approved which of the below is the most appropriate action to take?**

    A Resubmit the full prospectus

    B Withdraw the prospectus and do not resubmit for 21 days

    C Submit a supplementary prospectus for approval

    D Publish details in the media

30. **What does passporting relate to?**

    A It allows member firms of the EEA who have authorisation in one country to passport their business to another EEA country, subject to the restrictions of the FCA

    B It allows member firms of the EEA who have authorisation in one country to passport their business to another EEA country, subject to the restrictions of the MiFID

    C It allows member firms of the EU who have authorisation in one country to passport their business to another EU country, subject to the restrictions of the MiFID

    D It allows member firms of the EU who have authorisation in one country to passport their business to another EU country, subject to the restrictions of the FCA

31. **An investor owns 100,000 (£1 nominal value) ordinary shares in a listed company XYZ plc. The company has 10 million shares in issue. The table below shows the transactions made in XYZ plc shares by the same investor over a six-day period. On which of the days will disclosure be required under the Disclosure and Transparency Rules?**

Day 1	Buy	160,000
Day 2	Buy	70,000
Day 3	Sell	40,000
Day 4	Buy	80,000
Day 5	Buy	20,000
Day 6	Buy	50,000

    A Days 1, 2, 3 and 6

    B Days 2, 4 and 6

    C Days 1, 2, 4, 5 and 6

    D Days 2, 3, 4 and 6

32. **At what point must a bidder notify the market when they buy shares in the target company during a takeover bid?**

    A   Immediately

    B   By noon the next business day

    C   Within 24 hours

    D   By 08:30 the next business day

33. **All of the following are likely to result in a candidate failing the fit and proper criteria for an approved person, except:**

    A   Conviction for tax evasion

    B   Disclosed discharged bankruptcy

    C   Refusal of membership or licence to carry on a trade connected to financial services

    D   Censure by a regulator of financial services

34. **Which body is responsible for determining the suitability of a company for admission to AIM?**

    A   London Stock Exchange

    B   UK Listing Authority

    C   AIM Listing Authority

    D   Financial Conduct Authority

35. **Which of the following information does a company not need to disclose if it occurred after the prospectus was published, but before share dealing commenced?**

    A   That it is entering into discussions in relation to the possible sale of a subsidiary

    B   That is has just lost a contract covering 0.1% of turnover

    C   That its PBT is going to be 15% less than forecast

    D   A large transaction with a shareholder who holds 10% of the company's voting capital

36. **All of the following are legal requirements for a public limited company under Companies Act, except:**

    A   It has a minimum of two shareholders

    B   At least 25% of its nominal value and all the share premium must be paid up

    C   It must have a minimum issued share capital of £500,000

    D   The Memorandum of Association must state it is a plc

37. **All of the following are Takeover Code General Principles, except:**

    A   An offeror should only announce an offer once funding has been guaranteed

    B   All shareholders of the same class of an offeree company must be afforded equivalent treatment

    C   All parties to an offer must use every endeavour to prevent the creation of false markets

    D   Directors of an offeree must always act in the interests of the company as a whole

38. Which Act gives the FCA power to prosecute under Part V of the Criminal Justice Act 1993 for insider dealing offences or the prescribed regulations for money laundering offences?

A   Criminal Justice Act 1993

B   Financial Services and Markets Act 2000

C   Money Laundering Regulations 2003

D   Proceeds of Crime Act 2002

39. Which of the following are exempt from the requirement to seek authorisation from the FCA?

    I   Lloyd's

    II   Lloyd's members

    III LSE

    IV LSE members

A   I and II

B   I and III

C   II and III

D   II and IV

40. Who will issue a Decision Notice that declines the Part 4A permission for an authorised person?

A   The Enforcement Decisions Committee

B   The Discipline Decisions Committee

C   The Regulatory Decisions Committee

D   The Upper Tribunal

41. If a listed company makes an offer of £2.00 cash per share for another company's shares and during the offer period buys some of the offeree's shares in the market place for £2.10, then it will it be obliged to do all of the following, except:

A   Keep the offer open for at least a further 21 calendar days

B   Make an announcement of the purchase

C   Increase the offer to £2.10 per share for future acceptances

D   Increase the offer to £2.10 per share for offeree shareholders who have already accepted the offer at £2.00 a share

42. Which of the following is the least correct with respect to the FCA requirement for best execution?

A   The different execution venues to which an order can be directed must each be considered

B   The total consideration for a transaction should be considered

C   Specific client instructions should be ignored if they increase the price of the execution

D   The categorisation of the client must be considered

43. **All of the following must always be considered when assessing whether to re-classify a retail client as an elective professional client, except:**

    A His knowledge, experience and expertise

    B His ability to make his own investment decisions

    C His understanding of the risks involved

    D Meeting at least two of the criteria of the qualitative text

44. **Which TWO of the following are measures used in 'The Class Tests' to assess the materiality of a transaction?**

    I   Consideration test

    II   Current assets test

    III   Profits test

    IV   Turnover test

    A I and III

    B I and IV

    C II and III

    D II and IV

45. **All of the following must be stated in the Offer Document, except:**

    A The holdings of the offeror in the target company

    B The holdings of connected parties of the offeror in the target company

    C Any trades conducted by the offeror in the shares of the target company in the last three months

    D Any trades conducted by the offeror in the shares of the target company in the last 12 months

46. **What is the rule associated with the a 'break fee' that an offeree can offer to a recommended bidder?**

    A Break fees are not permitted without panel consent

    B A maximum break fee of 1% may be used without consent

    C A maximum break fee of 2.5% may be used without consent

    D A maximum break fee of 5% may be used without consent

47. **What is the first day on which an offeree shareholder can change their mind and withdraw their acceptance?**

    A Day 21

    B Day 39

    C Day 42

    D Day 46

48. **What is the consequence of a firm declining to make a holding announcement when it appears secrecy has been breached?**

    A The directors will be subject to up to two years' imprisonment for misleading the financial markets

    B Trading in the shares will be suspended

    C The company will be delisted

    D The firm will be subject to the disciplinary procedures set out in the Enforcement Sourcebook of the FCA Handbook

49. **Who has the responsibility to prepare an insider list?**

    A The FCA

    B The UKLA

    C The sponsor

    D The issuer

50. **In the FCA's Handbook of rules in relation to senior management controls, which of the following is true in relation to the need for apportionment?**

    A Systems should enable identification of risks

    B Records should be kept of senior management apportionment for three years

    C A list of the named directors for each responsibility should be maintained

    D The apportionment of responsibilities must be approved at the Annual General Meeting of the firm

Answers

1. **D** Money laundering is the process of hiding the true identity of illegally gained money. Making a profit from a drugs deal represents making illegal money as opposed to hiding its identity.

   See Chapter 1 Section 4.1 of your CISI Workbook

2. **C** Tradable debt (bonds) would be a specified investment; premium bonds are UK national Savings Bank investments and are not transferable.

   See Chapter 1 Section 1.5 of your CISI Workbook

3. **D** The MLRO (as required by the FCA) will commonly also take the role as the nominated officer as required by the money laundering regulations.

   See Chapter 1 Section 4.4 of your CISI Workbook

4. **A** Examination passes alone will not grant approval. The firm must also assess the individual as competent and the FCA must approve the application.

   See Chapter 1 Section 2.7.2 of your CISI Workbook

5. **C** Anyone who receives a Decision Notice from the RDC or FCA can refer the matter to the Tribunal, whether the recipient is the person who is the subject of the disciplinary case or a third party (such as their employer who will automatically receive a copy). The Tribunal can use all available evidence. However, the Tribunal is not part of the FCA structure and is within the remit of the Ministry of Justice.

   See Chapter 1 Section 2.11 of your CISI Workbook

6. **C** There are Principles of Market Conduct and Financial Prudence, but not the two combined.

   See Chapter 1 Section 2.2 of your CISI Workbook

7. **A** S 793 applies to all plcs, not just those which are listed.

   See Chapter 1 Section 3.7 of your CISI Workbook

8. **C** An issue denominated in amounts of £100k or more is likely to be of interest to professional investors only, who are capable of determining information about the issuer themselves without a prospectus.

   See Chapter 5 Section 1.1.2 of your CISI Workbook

9. **D** The FCA itself cannot wind up a company. It is a court that has the power to do this.

   See Chapter 1 Section 2 of your CISI Workbook

10. **A** When conflicts are not preventable through the firm's conflicts policy, the firm must disclose them to clients in sufficient detail for the client to take an informed decision.

    See Chapter 2 Section 5.1 of your CISI Workbook

11. **C** In a mandatory bid, the offeror must bid at the highest price they have bought at in the last 12 months.

    See Chapter 4 Section 2.11 of your CISI Workbook

12.   **A**   Large businesses are professional clients although they could be elective eligible counterparties.

See Chapter 2 Section 4.1.3 of your CISI Workbook

13.   **C**   Non-executive directors fulfil an advisory role and do not get involved in the day-to-day running of the company.

See Chapter 3 Section 1.2.1 of your CISI Workbook

14.   **D**   Personal account dealing rules do not apply to life policy personal transactions.

See Chapter 2 Section 6 of your CISI Workbook

15.   **B**   All of the options would be classified as a specified investment. However, only a unit in a collective investment scheme would meet the requirements of the narrower definition of a designated investment under the scope of the Conduct of Business Sourcebook.

See Chapter 1 Section 1.5 of your CISI Workbook

16.   **C**   The NOMAD is responsible for ensuring the AIM company complies with the Admission rules to AIM.

See Chapter 6 Section 2.4 of your CISI Workbook

17.   **B**   Reliance on others does not apply with regard to money laundering unless you have written confirmation that identification procedures have been performed by another firm, subject to the Money Laundering regulations.

See Chapter 1 Section 4.3.4 of your CISI Workbook

18.   **C**   A firm has a duty to assess suitability when it makes a personal recommendation (ie the client has asked for help).

See Chapter 2 Section 7.1 of your CISI Workbook

19.   **C**   The requirement is to specify the firm's name and address or contact point.

See Chapter 2 Section 3.2.1 of your CISI Workbook

20.   **C**   As the breach is by a commercial organisation, there cannot be a custodial sentence so the maximum penalty is an unlimited fine. An individual being found guilty may face up to ten years imprisonment plus a fine.

See Chapter 1 Section 4.6 of your CISI Workbook

21.   **A**   Financial promotions may be approved rather than issued by an authorised firm. E-mails are considered to be written financial promotions.

See Chapter 2 Section 3.1.1 of your CISI Workbook

22.   **C**   Although technically the BIS could prosecute, it is expected that the FCA will be the main prosecutor.

See Chapter 1 Section 5.2.2 of your CISI Workbook

23. **A** Establishing Chinese walls is just one method of managing a conflict under a conflicts of interest policy (not a policy of independence). Conflicts of interest do not only arise due to a firm acting as a market maker. Therefore, although the firm should avoid over-reliance on disclosure, this is the best available answer.

    See Chapter 2 Section 5.5 of your CISI Workbook

24. **C** An unlimited fine may be imposed as a penalty for committing Market Abuse. Public censures and restitution orders would also be possible.

    See Chapter 1 Section 7.3 of your CISI Workbook

25. **D** Sometimes, an approved person may be opted up to elective professional client. However, companies with a called up share capital of £5m or more are per se professional clients for non-MiFID business.

    See Chapter 2 Section 4.1.3 of your CISI Workbook

26. **B** SYSC refers to senior management arrangements, systems and controls requiring authorised firms to have adequate risk management systems and to take reasonable care to organise and control the affairs of the company responsibly.

    See Chapter 1 Section 2.5 of your CISI Workbook

27. **D** The use of Chinese walls is not obligatory although it is suggested that it is a good way to avoid conflicts of interest.

    See Chapter 2 Section 5.5 of your CISI Workbook

28. **A** Although the prospectus documents will contain financial accounts information, the Annual report and accounts is the annual document required for all companies.

    See Chapter 5 Section 1.3.3 of your CISI Workbook

29. **C** The supplementary proposal should be submitted for approval as soon as possible.

    See Chapter 5 Section 1.3.4 of your CISI Workbook

30. **B** Passporting covers the EEA. The MiFID regulates this activity.

    See Chapter 1 Section 8.2.7 of your CISI Workbook

31. **D** This relates to the disclosure requirement where shareholders must disclose their shareholdings as they reach 3% and, thereafter, whenever they go up or down through a full percentage point. Be careful to note the transaction on Day 3 is a sale and will therefore reduce the holding through a full percentage point.

    See Chapter 6 Section 1.8.1 of your CISI Workbook

32. **B** By noon on T+1. This is sometimes referred to as 'accelerated disclosure'.

    See Chapter 4 Section 2.10.1 of your CISI Workbook

33. **B** Both disclosed and undisclosed undischarged bankruptcy may result in a candidate being refused approved person status, but once discharged, this is less likely to prevent approval.

    See Chapter 1 Section 2.7.3 of your CISI Workbook

34. **A** The AIM market is an exchange-regulated market and so is not under the control of the UKLA and is effectively regulated by the LSE.

   See Chapter 6 Section 1.1.1 of your CISI Workbook

35. **B** The obligation for a company announcement is the same for listed companies as it is for those in the pre-list phase. Generally speaking, anything deemed to be price sensitive would need to be disclosed. It is unlikely that losing a relatively small contract is price sensitive but a drop in profits before tax of 15% would be.

   See Chapter 6 Section 1.5.2 of your CISI Workbook

36. **C** The minimum issued share capital is £50,000.

   See Chapter 1 Section 3.8 of your CISI Workbook

37. **A** Principle 5 merely states that an offer should only be made after ensuring any cash consideration can be fulfilled in full – it does not state that funding must be guaranteed. Equivalent treatment is Principle 1, false markets is Principle 4 and interests of whole company is Principle 3.

   See Chapter 4 Section 2.3 of your CISI Workbook

38. **B** The Financial Services and Markets Act 2000 gives the FCA power to prosecute under either the Criminal Justice Act 1993 regarding insider dealing offences or the Money Laundering Regulations/Proceeds of Crime Act 2002 in relation to money laundering offences. Note that the question is really asking where the FCA get their powers from, and the financial crime references are to distract you.

   See Chapter 1 Section 5.2.2 of your CISI Workbook

39. **C** Make sure you can differentiate between the Recognised Investment Exchange being exempt, whereas the RIE members require authorisation. Conversely, for the Lloyd's insurance market, 'The Society of Lloyd's' requires authorisation for arranging contracts of insurance, whereas the members of Lloyd's (called Names) who provide the risk capital are exempt.

   See Chapter 1 Section 1.7 of your CISI Workbook

40. **C** The RDC will issue the Decision Notice and the firm could then appeal to the Upper Tribunal, Tax and Chancery Chamber (TCCUT).

   See Chapter 1 Section 2.11 of your CISI Workbook

41. **A** The Takeovers Code has, as its first principle, the requirement to treat all shareholders equally. Therefore, it would not be fair to offer to some shareholders a higher price than others. An increased offer must be kept open for a further 14 calendar days.

   See Chapter 4 Section 2.3 of your CISI Workbook

42. **C** Clients must be warned that specific instructions could prevent the firm following its execution policy, but their execution instructions should be followed.

   See Chapter 2 Section 7.3 of your CISI Workbook

43. **D** There is no requirement to perform the quantitative test if it concerns non-MiFID business.

   See Chapter 2 Section 4.1.3 of your CISI Workbook

44.   **A**   The four class tests are gross assets, profits, consideration and gross capital.

See Chapter 6 Section 1.9.1 of your CISI Workbook

45.   **C**   The correct period for disclosure of trades by the offeror is 12 months. Therefore, although three months is within the 12 month period, the best answer is that transactions over 12 months must be disclosed.

See Chapter 4 Section 2.5.2 of your CISI Workbook

46.   **A**   Offering a break fee is no longer permitted unless the panel gives explicit consent.

See Chapter 4 Section 2.1 of your CISI Workbook

47.   **C**   The shareholder can change their mind on Day 42 provided the bid has not gone unconditional with regard to acceptances.

See Chapter 4 Section 2.16 of your CISI Workbook

48.   **B**   As some participants in the market may have inside information, the UKLA may consider it appropriate to suspend the shares.

See Chapter 6 Section 1.5.5 of your CISI Workbook

49.   **D**   It is the company itself who must maintain its own insider list.

See Chapter 6 Section 1.5.6 of your CISI Workbook

50.   **C**   Although systems should enable the identification of risk, this is not the specific need for apportionment asked for in the question. A list of apportioned responsibilities should be kept for six years.

See Chapter 1 Section 2.5.2 of your CISI Workbook

Practice Examination 5

(50 questions in 1 hour)

1. **Which of the following is not true regarding cold call financial promotions?**

    A   The call is permissible if it relates to controlled activities concerning readily realisable securities such as warrants

    B   Must make clear the purpose of call at the outset

    C   Must stop immediately if the customer is unwilling to proceed

    D   Clients are only called at an appropriate time of day

2. **Which of the following are exempt from the requirement to seek authorisation under s 19 FSMA?**

    I   Newspapers giving investment advice

    II   Cable TV programmes giving investment advice

    III   Trustees if they are not separately remunerated

    IV   Members of professional bodies where their main activity is not giving investment advice

    A   I and II

    B   I, II and IV

    C   IV only

    D   I, II, III and IV

3. **Which one of the following bodies with the role of investigating the effects of a merger or acquisition was formed by the Enterprise and Regulatory Reform Act 2013?**

    A   Office of Fair Trading

    B   Competition Commission

    C   Competition and Markets Authority

    D   Prudential Regulation Authority

4. **Which of the following is least likely to cause a conflict?**

    A   Encouraging customer A to sell so B can buy

    B   Recommending customer sells shares which analysts rate highly

    C   Customer buys shares where firm holds position

    D   Advising two customers in a takeover

5. **All of the following are true of the clients best interest rule, except:**

   A   A firm must act honestly, fairly and professionally in accordance with the best interest of its clients

   B   The rule applies to retail and professional clients in relation to MiFID business

   C   The rule applies to retail and professional clients in relation to non-MiFID business

   D   Fees, commissions and non-monetary benefits paid or provided to or by a third party must not impair the firm's duty to act in the best interest of the client

6. **A firm that has been granted Part 4A permission becomes:**

   A   A registered person

   B   An approved person

   C   A regulated firm

   D   An authorised person

7. **Which of the following is the best definition of passporting?**

   A   An authorised EEA firm passporting its authorisation into a Member State

   B   An EU firm passporting its authorisation into a Member State

   C   A FATF firm passporting its authorisation into a Member State

   D   An EEA firm opening a subsidiary in a Member State, having notified the regulator

8. **Which contains most UK money laundering legislation?**

   A   CJA 1993

   B   POCA 2002

   C   MiFID 2005

   D   FSMA 2000

9. **What is the maximum amount the FCA can fine an authorised company?**

   A   £100,000

   B   Nil, the FCA cannot fine

   C   £1,000,000

   D   Unlimited

10. **Which of the following would not breach s 177 of FSMA 2000?**

   A   Destroying documentation

   B   Failing to give documentation

   C   Intending to give misleading documentation

   D   Giving misleading documentation in good faith

11. **Which of the following is part of 'fit and proper' for an approved person?**

    A Membership of professional body

    B Financial soundness

    C Relevant experience

    D Membership of a regulatory body

12. **Which of the following are protected by Principle 10 on looking after investments?**

    A Retail clients only

    B Professional clients and retail clients only

    C Professional clients and eligible counterparties

    D All clients

13. **If an employee suspects money laundering activity, within what time period must they report their suspicions to their Money Laundering Reporting Officer?**

    A Immediately

    B As soon as is reasonably practicable

    C Within one business day

    D By the end of the current business day

14. **During a takeover, over what time period of the takeover timetable will an offer remain open?**

    A Between 14 and 21 days

    B Between 14 and 60 days

    C Between 21 and 60 days

    D Between 7 and 21 days

15. **Which of the following is false regarding obtaining a listing in the UK?**

    A Admission to listing is determined by the UKLA

    B The lower the level of free float, the higher the share price volatility

    C The minimum nominal value of shares to be listed is £700,000

    D No one major shareholder should prevent the company from operating independently

16. **Which one of the following is true in relation to Personal Account Dealing (PAD)?**

    A Records of PAD notification must be kept for six years

    B Employees must report transactions in life policies

    C PAD rules apply only to approved persons

    D A firm must ensure that any PAD transaction does not conflict with duties owed to clients

17. **Which of the following is false of an elective professional client?**

   A   The authorised firm must have a reasonable belief that the client is knowledgeable of the risks of the transactions

   B   The authorised firm must send a written warning of the protections that the client will lose

   C   The client must be knowledgeable in all activities that the firm is authorised to conduct

   D   The client must sign the written warning

18. **Which of the following is false with respect to FCA's investigatory powers under s 165?**

   A   Firms must comply immediately

   B   The request may be made by an agent of the FCA

   C   The FCA has statutory powers

   D   The FCA may require a skilled person's report

19. **A firm must take reasonable steps to apply the personal account rules to its employees, except in which one of the following cases?**

   A   The employee is an appointed representative

   B   The employee's activities consist only of own account transactions

   C   The employee is not involved in the firm's designated investment business

   D   The employee is carrying out a controlled function

20. **What percentage of an AIM float must be made available to the general public?**

   A   0%

   B   5%

   C   10%

   D   25%

21. **Which one of the following is true with regard to money laundering?**

   A   The Joint Money Laundering Steering Group Guidance Notes set out the FCA rules on money laundering prevention

   B   The maximum offence for assistance under POCA 2002 is seven years' imprisonment and an unlimited fine

   C   Identification of clients under the Money Laundering Regulations

   D   Employees of an FCA firm should report suspicions of money laundering to the National Crime Agency (NCA)

22. **Jane Doe is a junior research analyst with Howard & Sons, a brokerage and investment banking firm. Howard's mergers and acquisitions department, which handles mergers and acquisitions, has represented Britland Company in all its acquisitions for the past 20 years. Two of Howard's senior officers are directors of various Britland subsidiaries. Doe has been asked to write a research report on Britland. Based on the principles of business ethics, what is Doe's best course of action?**

   A   Doe may write the report provided the officers agree not to alter it

   B   Doe may write the report if she discloses Howard & Sons' special relationship with Britland in the report

   C   Doe may write the report but must refrain from expressing any opinions because of the special relationships between the two companies

   D   Doe should not write the report because the two Howard & Sons officers are 'constructive insiders'

23. **Big Company plc has just lost a significant contract. However, it is engaged in sensitive confidential discussions for a much larger contract that will more than compensate for the lost sales. What must Big plc disclose to the Regulatory Information Service?**

       I   As the new contract will compensate for the lost one no disclosure is required

       II   Details of the lost contract must be disclosed

       III   It may disclose details to its broker, if there is an agreement to keep it confidential

       IV   It may withhold details of the potential new contract

   A   I and IV

   B   II and IV

   C   I and III

   D   II and III

24. **SYSC Rule 3.1.1 covers the Principle for Business of:**

   A   Integrity

   B   Skill, care and diligence

   C   Management and control

   D   Communication with clients

25. **All of the following are true with relation to cold call promotions, except:**

   A   Calls should be made at an appropriate time

   B   The purpose of the call should be explained

   C   If the recipient does not wish to proceed then the call should be terminated

   D   Written confirmation of the call should be provided within five business days

26. **Which of the following is least likely to be considered a qualified investor with respect to prospectus rules?**

    A   A local authority

    B   A medium-sized company

    C   A self-certified private client who has experience, wealth and knowledge

    D   An authorised investment firm

27. **All of the following are considered to be key business ethics, except:**

    A   Integrity

    B   Transparency

    C   Confidentiality

    D   Objectivity

28. **An individual accused of insider dealing under CJA 1993 would least likely be able to defend himself with which of the following defences?**

    A   That he believed the information was already widely available such that it would make no material difference to the security price

    B   That he didn't expect to make a profit from the information

    C   That he would have acted irrespective of the information

    D   That he was unaware that the information was not widely available as he traded via a broker

29. **Which is the correct description of the offence of market abuse?**

    A   Criminal and punishable with fines and prison

    B   Civil and punishable with fines and prison

    C   Criminal and punishable with fines only

    D   Civil and punishable with fines only

30. **When may a MiFID firm passport its custody operations?**

    A   When it is also passporting its investment activities

    B   When it is also passporting its deposit taking activities

    C   When it is also passporting its underwriting services business

    D   When it is also passporting its corporate finance advisory activities

31. **Which one of the following transactions would not need to be reported to a listed company?**

    A   An individual owning 0.5% of a company acquires another 2.3%

    B   An individual owning 3.5% of a company acquires another 0.6%

    C   An individual owning 3.7% of a company disposes of 0.9%

    D   An individual owning 4.1% of a company disposes of 0.9%

32. **What is the minimum notice period usually required for an Annual General Meeting for a public company?**

    A   7 days

    B   14 days

    C   21 days

    D   28 days

33. **Which of the following is not covered by the CJA 1993 in relation to insider dealing?**

    A   Forward foreign exchange

    B   Debentures

    C   Option on shares

    D   American Depositary Receipts

34. **Under the UK Corporate Governance Code, which one of the following is false?**

    A   Remuneration of directors should be sufficient to attract, retain and motivate directors

    B   Remuneration should be set by an independent Audit Committee

    C   There should be a significant element of performance-related pay in directors' remuneration

    D   Notice periods for directors should not exceed one year

35. **What is the maximum penalty for a person found guilty of making a deliberately misleading statement to a client?**

    A   Unlimited fine

    B   Five years' imprisonment

    C   Seven years' imprisonment and an unlimited fine

    D   Five years' imprisonment and an unlimited fine

36. **Which instruments are covered by the insider dealing legislation?**

    I   Shares

    II   Bonds

    III   Options on shares

    IV   Depositary receipts

    A   I and II

    B   I, II, III and IV

    C   I, II and III

    D   I, II and IV

37. **Which two of the following are correct criteria for determining whether a cash alternative is required under the Panel rules?**

    I   In the case of any mandatory offer

    II When the offeror has purchased 10% or more of the company's share capital in the market for cash in the last 12 months

    III When the offeror has purchased 10% or more of the company's share capital in the last three months

    IV In the case of a mandatory offer only where the offeror has bought shares in the market in the last three months

    A   III and IV

    B   I and II

    C   I and III

    D   II and IV

38. **What proportion of the members, creditors, and debenture holders must consent to a scheme of reconstruction under the Companies Act?**

    A   Three quarters in value

    B   Majority in value

    C   Three quarters in number

    D   Majority in number and three quarters in value

39. **According to the COBS rule on conflicts of interest, an authorised firm should do which of the following?**

    A   Manage them fairly

    B   Decline to act

    C   Suspend the Chinese wall for that transaction

    D   Keep a record of the conflict

40. **Which of the following best describes an offer for subscription?**

    A   The company issuing shares sells the shares directly to the investors

    B   The company issuing shares sells the shares to an issuing house which sells the shares to investors

    C   The existing shareholders in the company sell shares directly to new investors

    D   The existing shareholders in the company sell shares to an issuing house which sells the shares to investors

41. **Which business would be subject to MiFID?**

    A   General insurance company

    B   Operator of an MTF

    C   Car insurance company

    D   Commodity trader

42. **It is least correct that one of the six listing principles says that a listed company must:**

    A   Deal with the FCA in an open and co-operative way

    B   Communicate with holders of its listed equity so as to avoid creation of a false market

    C   Ensure that listed securities are suitable for potential investors

    D   Act with integrity towards holders of its listed equity

43. **On launching a takeover bid, the bidder is required to circulate the announcement to all of the following, except:**

    A   Financial Conduct Authority

    B   Panel

    C   Employees of the target

    D   Employees of the bidder

44. **How long after the posting day must the first defence document be posted by?**

    A   14 calendar days

    B   14 business days

    C   21 calendar days

    D   21 business days

45. **The minimum price which must be offered by the offeror is the highest price they have paid for offeree shares during what period prior to the start of the offer period?**

    A   6 months

    B   3 months

    C   12 months

    D   1 month

46. **Which one of the following best describes the application of the Takeover Code?**

    A   It applies to all public limited companies that are registered in the UK, Channel Islands or Isle of Man that have securities trading on a UK regulated market (or stock exchange in the Channel Islands or Isle of Man)

    B   It applies to all listed companies that are registered in the UK, Channel Islands or Isle of Man that have securities trading on a UK regulated market (or stock exchange in the Channel Islands or Isle of Man)

    C   It applies to all public limited companies that are registered and managed in the UK, that have securities trading on a UK regulated market

    D   It applies to all public limited companies that have securities trading on a UK regulated market (or stock exchange in the Channel Islands or Isle of Man)

47. **Which one of the following is NOT one of the Listing Principles set out in the UKLA's Listing Rules in the FCA Handbook?**

A An issuer must take reasonable steps to establish and maintain adequate procedures, systems and controls to support the securities price for a maximum of 30 calendar days post-issue

B An issuer must act with integrity towards its current holders of listed equity securities

C An issuer must act with integrity towards its potential holders of listed equity securities

D An issuer must deal with the FCA in an open and co-operative manner

48. **All of the following are roles of the sponsor, except:**

A Satisfy itself that the issuer meets the requirements for listing

B Ensure that the issuer is properly guided and advised as to the application of the Listing Rules on an ongoing basis

C Support the trading of the security post issuance to provide sufficient liquidity in the secondary market

D Ensure that the issuer is properly guided and advised as to the application of the Disclosure Rules on an ongoing basis

49. **A period of ten days prior to the hearing of the UKLA to determine whether a security can be admitted to the full list, the issuer must submit all of the following documents, except:**

A Draft prospectus

B Request for authorisation to omit information normally required under the rules

C A statement from the sponsor that they accept responsibility for the accuracy of the information contained in the prospectus

D Copy of the Board resolution allotting the securities (or confirmation it will be provided within three days of approval)

50. **When preparing an insider list, which of the following is not required to be recorded?**

A The nature of the information held by each person

B The identity of each person having access to inside information

C The date the list was last updated

D The date the list was created

Answers

1.   **A**   The cold call may relate to readily realisable securities activities but it explicitly excludes warrants.

       See Chapter 2 Section 3.2.4 of your CISI Workbook

2.   **C**   Carefully read the question to note that it specifies **exempt** persons, not excluded. Media (newspapers, TV and radio) and unremunerated trustees are excluded, not exempt. As a memory technique, it may help to remember that excluded activities are those when there was no intention to regulate these people – they were just accidentally caught in the definition. Exempt persons are doing regulated activities, but they are regulated in another way than through FCA authorisation. In this case, lawyers, actuaries and accountants have their own professional regulators.

       See Chapter 1 Section 1.7 of your CISI Workbook

3.   **C**   The Competition and Markets Authority replaced the Office of Fair Trading and Competition Commission.

       See Chapter 4 Section 1.2.1 of your CISI Workbook

4.   **B**   Recommending an analyst's highly rated share is potentially bad advice but there is no obvious interest for the adviser or its clients and hence no evident conflict arising.

       See Chapter 2 Section 5.2 of your CISI Workbook

5.   **C**   The client best interest rule relates only to retail clients for non-MiFID business.

       See Chapter 2 Section 2.1.1 of your CISI Workbook

6.   **D**   Part 4A of FSMA relates to the scope of permission granted by the FCA for a firm to conduct a range of regulated activities. A 'person' in the context of authorisation relates to a firm or business and not an individual.

       See Chapter 1 Section 1.3.1 of your CISI Workbook

7.   **A**   Remember that passporting is covered throughout the EEA and hence is broader than just the EU. FATF stands for the Financial Actions Task Force and is not a regulator.

       See Chapter 1 Section 8.2.1 of your CISI Workbook

8.   **B**   The Proceeds of Crime Act 2002

       See Chapter 1 Section 4.1.1 of your CISI Workbook

9.   **D**   The FCA can impose unlimited fines on an authorised firm.

       See Chapter 1 Section 2.10.3 of your CISI Workbook

10.   **D**   Section 177 of FSMA 2000 states that it is a criminal offence to destroy and conceal information that could be relevant to an investigation. It is also an offence to knowingly provide misleading information. Acting in good faith would, therefore, not breach these conditions.

       See Chapter 1 Section 2.9 of your CISI Workbook

11. **B**   Although experience may be a consideration in assessing competence and capability, it is not in itself a requirement. However, financial soundness (eg not being an undischarged bankrupt) is an explicit requirement.

See Chapter 1 Section 2.7 of your CISI Workbook

12. **D**   The FCA's Principles for Businesses (excluding Principles 6 and 9 that only apply to customers) apply to all clients. All clients includes eligible counterparties.

See Chapter 1 Section 2.2 of your CISI Workbook

13. **B**   Failing to report suspicions as soon as is reasonably practicable is a criminal offence under the legislation.

See Chapter 1 Section 4.2 of your CISI Workbook

14. **C**   The takeover offer will always remain open as a minimum until at least Day 21, known as the first Closing Day. Then it may remain open up to a maximum of Day 60, known as the Final Day if the bidder wishes.

See Chapter 4 Section 2.16 of your CISI Workbook

15. **C**   If fewer shares are issued to the public (lower free float) then the share will be less liquid giving rise to bigger share price fluctuation (higher volatility). It is the minimum market value not nominal value which must be at least £700,000.

See Chapter 6 Section 1.4 of your CISI Workbook

16. **D**   Personal Account Dealing records must be kept for five years in relation to MiFID business and the rules apply to all employees doing designated investment business, not just approved persons. Trades in life policies are never likely to cause a conflict.

See Chapter 2 Section 6.1 of your CISI Workbook

17. **C**   A client will be an elective professional client just in specific areas.

See Chapter 2 Section 4.2.2 of your CISI Workbook

18. **A**   This question assumes you know that s 165 of FSMA covers the request for documents or information by the FCA surveillance inspector. This is a statutory, written notice that requires information to be produced within a reasonable period. It is the ability of the FCA to enter premises that is 'without notice'.

See Chapter 1 Section 2.9 of your CISI Workbook

19. **C**   Personal Account Dealing rules apply only to designated investment business.

See Chapter 2 Section 6 of your CISI Workbook

20. **A**   There is no minimum free float for AIM shares.

See Chapter 6 Section 2.8 of your CISI Workbook

21. **C**   The FCA rules on money laundering are set out in SYSC. The maximum penalty under POCA 2002 is 14 years' imprisonment and an unlimited fine. Employees of a firm should report suspicions to their MLRO and not directly to the NCA (formerly SOCA).

See Chapter 1 Section 4.3.2 of your CISI Workbook

22. **B** The principles of integrity and objectivity should still allow her to write the report including her opinions, but professional behaviour best practice would require her to disclose this interest, as would the COBS rules on conflicts of interest.

See Chapter 2 Section 5.3.2 of your CISI Workbook

23. **B** The directors have a general duty to disclose all information necessary to appraise investors of the company's positions and to avoid a false market in its shares.

See Chapter 6 Section 1.5.2 of your CISI Workbook

24. **C** Firms must have **appropriate** management systems and controls.

See Chapter 1 Section 2.2 of your CISI Workbook

25. **D** Written confirmation is not required.

See Chapter 2 Section 3.2.4 of your CISI Workbook

26. **B** A medium-sized company would not be a qualified investor unless they self-certify as such.

See Chapter 5 Section 1.1.2 of your CISI Workbook

27. **B** Transparency is a key attribute of markets where we should be able to see what is happening to prices.

See Chapter 3 of your CISI Workbook

28. **D** Believing that the information was not widely available just because the individual traded through a broker does not make any sense. The other three answers are general defences set out in the Criminal Justice Act.

See Chapter 1 Section 5.3 of your CISI Workbook

29. **D** Market abuse is a civil offence and as such there is no prison sentence.

See Chapter 1 Section 7.1 of your CISI Workbook

30. **A** Custody operations are ancillary services and may only be passported in conjunction with services, which are dealing in investments, managing investments, arranging the receipt and transmission or orders, advising on investments and operating a MTF.

See Chapter 1 Section 8.2.3 of your CISI Workbook

31. **A** They are all movements through a full percentage point of 3% or higher and are thus reportable under the Disclosure and Transparency Rules, except for A which remains below the 3% threshold.

See Chapter 6 Section 1.8.1 of your CISI Workbook

32. **C** A notice period of 21 days is usually required for an **AGM for a public company**.

See Chapter 1 Section 3.6.1 of your CISI Workbook

33. **A** CJA 1993 only applies to securities and related derivatives on securities and therefore could not be applied to a currency deal.

See Chapter 1 Section 5.1 of your CISI Workbook

34. **B** The directors' pay awards are set by a Remuneration Committee made up of non-executive directors.

    See Chapter 3 Section 1.2.4 of your CISI Workbook

35. **C** The criminal offences which relate to making misleading statements and practices carries a maximum possible sentence of seven years and an unlimited fine.

    See Chapter 1 Section 6.1 of your CISI Workbook

36. **B** Criminal Justice Act 1993 covers trading in shares, debt securities issued by the private or public sector, warrants, depositary receipts, options, futures or contracts for difference (CFDs) on any of the foregoing.

    See Chapter 1 Section 5.1 of your CISI Workbook

37. **B** There must be a cash alternative for any mandatory offer and where 10% or more has been bought for cash in the last year.

    See Chapter 4 Section 2.11 of your CISI Workbook

38. **D** It is both the majority by number and three quarters in value that is required. For shareholders we will assume that they all have the same nominal value share and so number and value are equal, but for creditors we need a simple majority in number together with three quarters in value.

    See Chapter 4 Section 2.17 and Chapter 1 Section 3.1 of your CISI Workbook

39. **A** Principle 8 requires that when conflicts arise, the firm manages the conflict to ensure that customers are treated fairly.

    See Chapter 1 Section 2.2 of your CISI Workbook

40. **A** Compared to the offer for sale, where the issuing house sells shares on behalf of the company and existing members.

    See Chapter 6 Section 1.7.1 of your CISI Workbook

41. **B** The operators of MTFs are covered by MiFID, while insurance companies and commodity traders are not.

    See Chapter 1 Sections 8.2.3 and 8.2.5 of your CISI Workbook

42. **C** The listed firm is not required to ensure that securities are suitable for investors.

    See Chapter 2 Section 5 of your CISI Workbook

43. **A** The FCA is not directly involved in the regulation of takeover and merger activities in the UK.

    See Chapter 4 Section 1 of your CISI Workbook

44. **A** All days in the Blue Book are calendar days.

    See Chapter 4 Section 2.16 of your CISI Workbook

45. **B** This requirement falls under Rule 6 of the Takeover Code.

    See Chapter 4 Section 2.9 of your CISI Workbook

46. **A**   The full definition is not concerned with listing status or where the company is managed, but does require the securities to be traded on a regulated market.

   See Chapter 4 Section 2.1 of your CISI Workbook

47. **A**   There is no requirement for the price to be stabilised post issuance.

   See Chapter 6 Section 1.4 of your CISI Workbook

48. **C**   The role of providing liquidity in the secondary market would be that of a stabilisation manager immediately post issuance and a market maker on an ongoing basis.

   See Chapter 1 Section 5.3.2 of your CISI Workbook

49. **C**   It is the directors of the issuer who must accept ultimate responsibility for the prospectus.

   See Chapter 5 Section 1.3.2 of your CISI Workbook

50. **A**   The rules require the reason why the person is on the list to be recorded but does not need to specify the exact information held.

   See Chapter 6 Section 1.5.6 of your CISI Workbook